Discovering Treasure Within

A New and Comprehensive Tool

for Spiritual Direction

R. Carroll Travis

Illustrated by Joanna Johnson

The Kingdom of Heaven is like treasure hidden in a field;
someone stumbled upon it and covered it up. Then with joy
the finder goes, sells everything, and buys that field.
Matthew 13:44

A Maple Creek Media Publication

Printed in the United States of America

ISBN-13: 978-1-937004-21-7
ISBN-10: 1-937004-21-X

The opinions, beliefs, and viewpoints contained in this publication are expressed solely by the author and do not necessarily reflect the opinions, beliefs and viewpoints of Maple Creek Media or Old Line Publishing, LLC. Maple Creek Media and Old Line Publishing are not responsible for the accuracy of any of the information contained in this publication.

Cover Design: Nell K.T. Campbell

Maple Creek Media is a division of Old Line Publishing, LLC

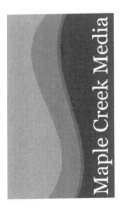

Maple Creek Media
c/o Old Line Publishing, LLC
P.O. Box 624
Hampstead, MD 21074
Toll-Free Phone: 1-877-866-8820
Toll-Free Fax: 1-877-778-3756
Email: info@maplecreekmedia.com
Website: www.maplecreekmedia.com

The spiritual journey to become fully alive will not be about self-improvement, but about self-fulfillment. It will not develop the ego; but it will manifest the true self by cooperation with divine grace. It will be about choosing to be the person God is calling into being and finally to behold God face to face.

Acknowledgements

Excerpts from John Mains, "In the Stillness Dancing;" Antoine de Saint -Exupery, "The Little Prince;" H.B Dehquani-Tafti, "The Hard Awakening;" and Fr. Andrew, "The Life and Letters of Father Andrew" are gratefully reprinted by permission of the publishers.

The detail from Jan Van Eyck, "The Arnolfini Marriage," is reprinted by arrangement with Art Resources NY. Other images on the CD-ROM are in the Public Domain; many thanks to those who have shared resources on Wikimedia Commons. Thanks also to the Department of Christian Education of The Orthodox Church in America for use of several line drawings of icons by Fr. John Matusiak from their resources web-site.

Special thanks go to sound engineers H.E. Beckner and F.J. Bailey; and also to Fr. Peter Roberts and the people of St. Luke's Episcopal Church, Merritt Island, FL for graciously allowing the author to use their organ to record background for the audio-meditations.

The Scripture quotations contained herein are from the New Revised Standard Version Bible, copyright@1989 by the Division of Christian Education of the National Council of the Churches of Christ in the U.S.A., and are used by permission. All rights reserved.

Thanks also must be extended to Craig Schenning of Old Line Publishing and Maple Creek Media for yeomanly work and always helpful advice; to Nell K.T. Campbell for her cover design; and to inspired illustrator Joanna Johnson for the copyrighted drawings she made to introduce each section of the book.

And most of all thanks to Karen, the love of my life and always my inspiration.

Contents

IN THIS BOOK

ON THE CD-ROM

I. Audio Meditations:

1. *Water of Life,* C. Debussy, "La Cathedrale engloutie"

2. *The Wonderful Cube,* J. Alain, "Le Jardin Suspendu"

3. *An Encounter with Christ the Youth,* M. Ravel, "Pavane"

4. *Meditation on Christ the Hero (2),* E. Satie, "Gymnopedie

5. *Tree of Life,* A. Guilmont, "Priere"

6. *The Transformation,* A. Copland, "Simple Gifts Variations"

7. *Meeting the Risen Savior on the Beach,* W.A. Mozart, "Ave Verum Corpus"

O. Messiaen, two of "Seven Short Visions: Les Corps Glorieux"

8. "Joy and Clarity of the Glorified Bodies"

9. "Force and Agility of the Glorified Bodies"

10. *The Heart's Deepest Desire,* E. Elgar, "Nimrod" from "The Enigma Variations"

11. *The Soul's Garden,* M. Ravel, "Pavane"

12. *Six Moments with Christ,* G. Mahler, "Adagietto" from "Symphony No. Four"

II. Images to View, Print or Upload
(Public Domain, excepting #18)

1. "The Virgin of the Sign" (icon), Kizhi Monastery, 18th Century

2. "The Annunciation to Mary" (icon), Ohrid, early 14th Century

3. "Emmanuel" (icon), Simon Ushakov, 1668

4. "Christ with the Elders in the Temple" (icon), Novgorod, 16th Century

5. "The Temptation of Christ in the Wilderness," Simeon Holmojorec, 1682

6. "The Three Temptations" (mosaic icon), San Marco, Venice, 12th Century

7. "Christ the Pantocrator" (icon), St. Catherine's Monastery, 4th Century

8. "Christ Enthroned, the Teacher" (icon), Novgorod, 16th Century

9. "Tree with Roots by the Water," Word Press

10. "The Crucifixion of Our Lord" (icon), Novgorod, 1360

11. "Anastasis" (fresco), Chora Church, Istanbul, 1315-1321

12. "Adam and Eve" (engraving), Albrecht Durer, 1504

13. "Adam and Eve" (painting), Lucas Cranach the Elder, 1526

14. "Echo and Narcissus" (painting), John William Waterhouse, 1903

15. "The Kiss" (painting), Gustave Klimt, 1907/08

16. "The Conversation" (painting), Henri Matisse, 1908-1912

17. "The Arnolfini Marriage" (painting), Jan Van Eyck, 1422

18. Mirror Detail from "The Arnolfini Marriage" –licensed by Art Resources, NY

19. "Hercules and Deianira" (painting), Jan Gossart (Mabuse), 1517
20. "The Embrace of St. Anne and St. Joachim" (icon), 2000
21. "Burial of the Count of Orgaz" (painting), El Greco, 1586
22. "Basil the Blessed" (bas relief), St. Basil's Church, Moscow, 16th Century
23. "Blessed Basil and John of Moscow" (icon), Anton Rublev, 17th Century
24. "The Presentation of Christ in the Temple" (icon), Novgorod, 15th Century

III. Seasonal Series:

Five detailed session plans, adapted from the book, with publicity resources

Resources: Notice or Handout Model, Evaluation
Session I: "Exploring Inner Space – Journaling and Sharing"
Session II: "Dream Work"
Session III: "Phases of the Archetype of Christ"
Session IV: "God's Power to Hold and Lead"
Session V: "Encounter With Jesus the Savior"

INTRODUCTION

FULLY ALIVE NOW

TAKING THE PLUNGE

The glory of God is the human person fully alive;
and, the life of humanity is the vision of God.
~St. Irenaeus~

Stooping and poking one hand into the water under the Mackinac Island Bridge, the swimmer reconsidered. Someone remarked the waters of Lake Superior are so cold she never gives up her dead. And now there was firsthand evidence.

Several wild swans glide just off shore, making wakes that blend as they move briskly along. The air is fresh with the aroma of evergreens that develops when the sun is strong. It must be nearly noon. There will never be a better time than summer at noon; later in the day the air will be as chilling as the water. The swimmer is one of those hardy souls who need to experience things – a visceral type. Sure, the water was great on a Caribbean reef skimming along with schools of brightly colored fish. Even the hotel pools aren't bad when large enough to do a few laps. The swimmer has sometimes filed trips mentally under: "How was the water?" But the prospect of swimming with the sturgeons of the Great Lakes requires more commitment than usual. Wading out into the frigid surf is clearly not the way to test these waters: *I'll always regret not taking the plunge.* So the swimmer does just that.

The rush of shocking cold takes away the breath. It is hard to stop the reflexive urge to inhale before breaking the surface. But with only seconds of gliding, then moving along faster with a sharp frog-kick, a hard pull of the arms takes over by habit. The swimmer begins to think happily of the speedy burn of calories to cope with a hearty, north woods breakfast, and relaxes into the familiar crawl; rhythmic breathing side to side takes over.

The whole body tingles. The swimmer senses the edges of muscles never noticed before. It is startling to the whole system, as cold penetrates beyond the top layers of skin, something a seal or penguin would never know. But for a human, this exhilarating sensation is full of aspiration, like what motivates us to explore space or plumb dark caverns in the earth. With deep breathing comes a zone of gliding relaxation- efficient, like the swans up ahead, using only minimal energy. The swimmer relaxes for a bit into an experience both familiar and new; then sprints back to shore, and pushes upright out of the water like a released spring. Arms stretch wide into the warming noonday; nose opens to an intense burst of pine-scented air.

The swimmer's whole being somehow expands into a moment of celebration: *Oh! The freshness of being fully alive!*

++++++++++

This little story is a metaphor for something felt by everyone as both a problem and a remote possibility, for something desirable yet challenging, and always resisted as a risk to the status quo.

To be fully alive, this is our deep desire, but how to get there? We might pursue adventure or excitement, as in the story; but more often we just try rearranging the surface of life. We vow to take control of our diet and exercise. Perhaps we mull over a job change, or a vacation. Some read and practice the advice of a currently touted self-help plan. Others might search for the right life partner, or seek a vibrant religious community to stave off loneliness. But most often something foils the intent to improve things. One may feel trapped in a genetically chunky body that never measures up to whatever ideal. It becomes clear that no one could run far enough or fast enough to escape our stressors. When the big trip comes up, it rains all week in paradise. The church we sought out has its own problems, and the music is annoying. The career path we sacrificed so much to enter shows signs of becoming a dead end. The new spouse turns out to have variations on the behavior of the former one. Somehow no fresh paint or rearrangement of the furniture ever makes life's dwelling what we hoped for. We slog through long stretches of disillusionment.

Since there are so many choices available, it may take years to realize little that is truly satisfying can develop while moving along the surface of life's trends and temporary satisfactions in pursuit of happiness. Realizing this, we may become even more firmly entrenched in the plodding routines of an ordinary life tinged with hopelessness. But a voice inside still whispers "Is this all there is?"

Of course this ordinary, responsible life with its sprinkle of rewards – a reliable vehicle, and a nice home and well-fed family - is in some ways the *ideal* pursued vigorously by most of the world's struggling people. For a recovering addict, *normal* is the dimly perceived hope for sobriety. It is the never-land of those who can't seem to grow into their responsibilities. It is the wish to be normal that challenges those who see themselves as too short, too tall, or too something else, and also those who are impaired by genes or circumstances. So many of us are struggling with dysfunction or deprivation that the urge to be normal may offer enough motivation to keep us plodding along, at least getting by. Is there any real hope of living fully when so many obstacles seem insurmountable?

And when all the stories are told, is there anything more to expect than survival while treading the turbulent waters of grief, disillusionment or frustration? Or to consider an even more perilous possibility, when the waters are calm and the weather decent, will we waste opportunities while skimming back and forth from one transient pleasure to another? Perhaps, but then a stormy crisis, disease or some other circumstance, forces us to attend to a more challenging situation in a new way. For a while we may even anchor in genuine spirituality. But we inevitably return to the old habitual way - unless we find and persevere in what has come to be called an "effective spiritual practice."

To sustain a spiritually grounded life, various disciplines need to be carefully chosen and practiced. Life's challenges will have better outcomes for those who work with a set of tools such as reflection and imagination, and also exhibit qualities of character such as perseverance and courage. Above all, we will want to have a core relationship of dynamic intimacy with God. To use the imagery of St. Theresa of Avila, the early phases of spiritual growth may raise blisters, as when carrying water in buckets to a parched field; still, with effort, the fields are watered. But, with the development of such disciplines as are proposed in this book, there will be tools that allow the deeper waters to flow more from within, as through an irrigation system. Eventually life will come full circle, though not to *childishness* which is passive and self-centered; rather to *childlikeness*, because it includes full involvement of the adult faculty of choice. And as one's spiritual practice matures, the gentle rains of God's love are likely to produce fruit with even less effort on our part.

The writer of Psalm 131 commends a disciplined, calm and trusting inner state of mature childlikeness: **I do not occupy myself with great matters, or things that are too hard for me. But I still my soul and make it quiet, like a weaned child upon its mother's breast; my soul is quieted within me** (Ps. 131: 2-3). And so, let us acknowledge that spiritual growth is always, and with increasing freedom, a matter of choice. More and more the choice must be ours, not that of even the best parents. God gives us the ability to choose fuller life: **For freedom Christ has set us free; stand fast, therefore, and do not submit again to a yoke of slavery** (Galatians 5:1). Always the choice will be at hand. This book will encourage you to make well-informed daily choices to become more fully alive; and it will provide you with insights and tools to help you continue to grow.

Living fully is not just a goal, but an opportunity to make better choices continually, based on expanding awareness. The **Now** of the chapter title does not indicate instant success or short-cuts, but that the joyous person we are becoming is already present, seeking to emerge and act. A fuller, richer life is also within reach whenever we are challenged by circumstances. But desperation or crisis is not required to locate the joy. It is always possible to choose freely what will bring greater vitality now and for the future. The method explored here presents a well-tested way to live that only gets better with practice. This is, of course, an enormously idealistic claim. It is based on the confidence of the early Christians, who were on to something powerful and wonderful. There is One dwelling among us who has come **that they may have life, and have it abundantly** (John 10:10). For centuries in different cultures and challenging situations, there have been many to bear witness to God's good news: **the same yesterday, today and forever** (Hebrews 13:8). The apostle Paul discovered and proclaimed: **The mystery hidden…now made manifest to his saints: Christ in you, the hope of glory** (Colossians 1:26-27). The good news is that we are able to make such a joyful discovery part of our story every day; what seems ordinary can be affirmed and become an occasion for joy. By inner transformation we become **fully alive now.**

THE METHOD: JOURNALING

To reflect in a journal, whether on a computer or with pen and paper, can be a potent spiritual exercise. Once a reflection is written, it will have a life of its own. What is put down in words seems to be from another self, *me-reflecting.* How wonderful it can be to practice a way to listen to oneself deeply! Within a short period the user's own experience should demonstrate the value of this method. Reading over past reflections can inspire fresh explorations and later insights. Just thinking about the questions and exercises to come will not be the same or as powerful as journaling. And the written method should still be used when there will be sharing with another or with a group.

The following chapters are designed to prepare for written personal reflection, not necessarily to be shared within a group. If a group is formed, or if the book is used with a spiritual friend or mentor, some sections may be shared with discussion afterwards. This must be done with permission and respect for the privacy of all participants. It is always helpful to listen to the experience of others. Certainly to hear one's own experience in a fresh way by sharing it in a group of trusted friends will add another dimension. But most users of this material will likely practice journaling privately, over a period of time. Not everything written could or should be shared.

If this work is used with a small group, a leader - probably a pastor or counselor - should schedule and organize the sessions and assure confidentiality: one who will complement the author's role as spiritual friend and be a companion on the journey.

In a spiritual journal, the primary audience is the Holy Spirit, who will always be "at your side and on your side" – the Paraclete. The Spirit always listens with great discretion, to the unsaid movements of each heart, to bring energy and encouragement. He is like the best psychotherapist imaginable, always involved and assisting each person to explore the depths in order to come to fullness of life. Before each session, take a few moments to be quiet and pray, "Come Holy Spirit..." Do this in your own welcoming way. You can expect to be infused with deeper peace and joy.

FOUR INITIAL JOURNALING EXERCISES: ATTITUDE ADJUSTMENT

For coming to be "fully alive," an appropriate attitude will be essential, like a good pair of walking shoes: a prepared and equipped character you can rely on for the long haul. It will be necessary from time to time, to check your basic attitude; and if needed, to stop long enough to recover the conditions for an effective journey. A poor attitude will not make the trip impossible, only more difficult. A spiritual mentor should be able to keep these conditions in place.

Here follows what this writer thinks are the four most important elements of a good attitude for spiritual growth. These elements are within each of us in some form, and can be brought to the surface by noticing what comes to mind and then reflecting in a journal. There will be a blank space for a further reflection, in case you decide something essential is missing from the list. If the journey is to be alone, write a series of reflections to start your journal on the baseline attitudes with which you have begun, and return to it from time to time to clarify, revise, or simply to check the "equipment." If you are working with a supportive small group, you may find it helpful in the first session or just before to write your reflections and then share parts of them. To get better acquainted, discuss your reactions and thoughts about the four conditions outlined below. Then decide together about any missing essentials.

Attitude 1: *Availability*

This is all about willingness to proceed. Am I willing to be a pilgrim reaching out to the unknown within and without? (It can be helpful to look at one's usual excuses, and then to decide if the reasons are important or not.) All the stories in the Gospels in which Jesus calls disciples to "Follow me," seem to involve leaving something specific behind. One potential follower said he must first go and bury his father. Jesus' response was startling: "Let the dead bury the dead." Who knows how the conversation went from there? Or, what was the outcome? The Gospel of John's last chapter has a question repeated three times: "____do you love me?" There follows each time "Feed my sheep," and then the invitation, "Follow me." Our spiritual availability may be strong, weak or distracted by other priorities. We need to be continually aware of this part of our attitude. The answer to "Am I available?" may shift frequently among options like "yes, no, maybe or later." Explore what your answer means. This is essential because cooperation requires freedom. "Where the Spirit of the Lord is, there is freedom." Check the limits of your availability from time to time and sit with this question in prayer. To be "fully alive," will ultimately have to mean being fully available to One who is "the Lord and giver of life."
   Journaling Question: In what ways am I, and am I not available?

Attitude 2: *Willingness to Change Behavior*

To be influenced by the Spirit depends on being willing to make changes. The changes required are usually small: "What is necessary to take the next step?" Still, a person must be willing, or as one spiritual director puts it, "willing to be willing." Normally there will be a degree of inner resistance to moving along to spiritual maturity. The issue here is free obedience. This means people who move efficiently along in the spiritual journey will become flexible to changes of course, malleable to the shaping of circumstances in life, but not all at once. To test this, sit in prayer in silence before God with the question, "In this situation, what can I do to please you?" Some will find the familiar Serenity Prayer helpful in this attitude check. "Lord, grant me the ability to change what I can, to acknowledge what cannot be changed, and grant me the wisdom to know the difference."

Journaling Question: Am I willing to take the next small step? What is this step?

Attitude 3: *Hopefulness*

Hope, as St. Paul established, is an abiding condition –a chosen (not necessarily felt) positive orientation toward what is to come. We need to live with it all the time or else often the right behavior will take root but fail to thrive. Since it is impossible to "work up" hope, we should pray for this basic attitude. Though it is always a spiritually positive movement into the unknown future, hope is hard to describe; yet its presence or lack is always recognizable. Perhaps Emily Dickenson's well-known image is a sufficient definition: "Hope is the thing with feathers that perches on the soul." The absence of hope is easy to spot. Look for cynicism, despair, ennui and such behaviors as self-medication and empty pastimes. None of these conditions is to be desired once we recognize them. When these things come up, be aware, let them go, and then ask for the renewing attitude of hope. **Seek, and you will find** *(Matthew 7:7).*

Journaling Question: Do I have a hopeful attitude right now? What is this like for me?

Attitude 4: *Pursuing a True Vision*

"The life of the human person," Irenaeus wrote, "is the vision of God." *This may seem abstract, but it fixes the direction we want to move on the spiritual journey. Since we cannot now see the destination, we must learn to continually follow the signs pointing to the goal. This is why it is critical to learn to seek Jesus' presence, en-fleshed in the world. Jesus said,* **I am the way, the truth and the life. No one comes to the Father except by me** *(John 14:6). If we aren't sure who we are following, it may be "the blind leading the blind." There is an account of a large group of cross country runners who followed the pack when a respected runner missed a directional sign. Only four turned onto the right path. One of these paused, waving and pointing the way; but it was to no avail as the pack whizzed by, some laughing. Needless to say, only those four finished the race. The Spirit of God has carefully placed signs along our path. Do we really know where we are headed? Can we spot, and are we following the correct signs? St. Paul reminds us:* **You compete for an imperishable crown. So run that you may win** *(I Corinthians 9:24). Winning spiritually is not about finishing in first place; it is about staying on course and persevering.*

Journaling Question: At this time, and looking back on my experience, what signs do I see pointing toward my ultimate victory?

Attitude 5: *The Open Question*

The four elements above, in the considered opinion of this writer, are the essential components of a right attitude for the spiritual journey. But this analysis may not be correct or sufficient. If something seems missing and calls out to you like a flashing neon sign, consider this seriously. Take time to define what is missing and discuss or write a journal entry about it.

BEFORE TAKING THE PLUNGE

The flow of chapters to come follows the natural progression of our life cycle. There is a composite of inner imagery, like the phases of the moon, which represents for each of us the whole range of human experience - something Carl Jung referred to as *archetypal*. But these spiritual realities have a non-temporal character. After an overview of the archetypes, an entirely different order of progression may suggest itself. Don't hesitate to change the order. For example, a period of creativity or some new undertaking may bring the *child* phase of the archetype to the forefront, bringing with it fresh insights and rejuvenating energy to accomplish something new. This experience could happen to a person chronologically far from childhood. Contact with the eternal also produces moments of recurring meaning through recovered memory. The spiritual journey can be organized thematically as well a sequentially. Note as well that the issues of aging and maturity are not just relevant to persons older in years. Every important event, after all, has its moment of decline. And every seedling contains its full flower of possibility. Once overviewed, the chapters should be used in whatever order seems right for the moment, or chapters may be used individually and separately as needed.

It may also be helpful to survey the design common to each chapter. First there will be a line drawing suggestive of the archetypal phase to be explored, followed by a brief story. Each narrative outlines dilemmas and possibilities, conflicts and resolutions inherent in the subject matter. The stories, more like vignettes, contain the themes to be explored. Then follows a section focusing on a specific scriptural passage that reveals a phase of the heroic Christ, and then exposition will draw out some emotional and spiritual implications. Finally there are throughout, questions and exercises for journaling, and sometimes for sharing. These responses are interspersed with various meditative presentations to stimulate your own reflection.

The accompanying CD provides additional resources of music, art and an audio version of most meditations. It is impossible to read and meditate at the same time, so listening to the CD will be very helpful, even for groups. The color prints may be downloaded and projected or copied. All images are in the Public Domain (except for a detail from "The Arnolfini Marriage," licensed for use with permission). Leaders will also find a full set of lesson plans for a five-week introductory series; this might be ideal for Advent or Lent.

Discovering the Treasure Within

CHAPTER ONE

THE PRIMAL EGG: NEW LIFE

KEVIN & HIS EGG

There is an Irish tale from the days when men and women both were tough and saints truly vigorous. Kevin was a man of prayer renowned for discipline and perseverance. When the Lenten fast came near, the simple monk took stock of what he might need to sustain him for the season. Deciding to take only the holy Word of God and his homespun garment, he set off into the deep woods to seek solitude. Far out and half way up a hill he reached a clear place that felt inviting. Turning around he considered the expanse of valley, also friends and consolations he must leave behind. He settled down, resting his back against the rough bark of a chosen tree. Leather-bound book in one hand, the other lying palm upward and open upon the mossy ground, he was at peace. He sensed the warm spring sunshine on his skin. Kevin felt a certain poise in this situation, and resolved to stay here in complete stillness. Perhaps God would stir some new life in him, just as a seed resting in the soil would burst its shell to push a new green shoot out from within itself.

The monk had almost forgotten his earthly body when he caught a glimpse of downy feathers and moss upon the upturned palm and fingers of his hand. With a single movement of the eyes, he noticed a small black bird lining his open hand with great care. And then she nestled there, quiet as the patient monk. Eventually he felt the slight pressure of a mottled egg, warm from the mother bird. The moment he became fully aware of this, she hopped off and flew away without chirp or song. Kevin concluded that in this small wonder, the Creator had placed an Easter blessing softly upon him, full of the power of fresh life. And he resolved to wait.

As light increased, the days warmed, grass grew up, and the buds ripened in the forest all around. Kevin became more and more focused on what he had become: a nest. As he gave himself over to bringing forth a particular feathered life, he wondered how his mother felt bringing him to birth within her body. His intent sharpened as the holy fast drew on. He busied his mind upon the Psalms and Gospels like fingers upon a harp. His body was becoming what this circumstance had called for it to be. The egg seemed smooth and lifeless as stone, yet warm. The saint hoped that in due time, a tiny beak might peck away the shell. When the chick eventually declared itself with a coarse "cheep", the monk knew the arrival of Easter Day would not suffice. He must remain until, fed by daily visits of the blackbird, the chick would fly away. After a time of hopping around and returning to the fingered nest, the new bird found the power in its wings and flew.

Meanwhile the saint's heart became intensely pure, though of course he scarcely noticed that. It was fully Pentecost when Kevin returned to the valley and to life with his kin and brethren. He joined them in cultivating the summer fields and offering up the endless canticle of praise.

JOURNALING EXERCISE

This will be an interactive journey, actually an inner pilgrimage. You might want to sleep on the dreamlike story of St. Kevin, the ascetical super-hero. See if God has conspired with nature to lay a particular "egg" in your life. (You may even discover other eggs placed with you that went unnoticed, without a soul to care for them and reap the benefits.) It may be your awareness is quite scattered, with little sense of what new things might be coming within reach. Or you may discover a need to be still, to permit the circles of disturbance to settle on the pond of your imagination before locating the newness in your life. Or maybe you can do this, but you have developed a habit of automatically pushing aside whatever seems strange or inconvenient. To grow, one must find, like Kevin, a desire to persevere. Eventually, in its own time, you will note the delicate shell of *something* placed just so, within your reach. At first you may detect only the shell. But there will be time enough to help whatever's inside to break out, and to accept and care for this new life until it matures. For the moment, just be attentive to whatever strange but natural thing God will cause to be.

When you are ready to get started with this inner project, settle down for a bit in a quiet place, and rest crossed palms in your lap facing upward. Don't bother with the over-the-top process of forming a "nest". Relax and let the stress drain from your body. Slowly and deeply inhale, pause and exhale. Imagine a warm fresh egg is placed in your palm. Let the image develop, using all five senses in whatever order seems natural to you. Then moving on, let this image go and wait for signs of new life to emerge. Patiently and without judgment, look at the idea this egg seems to represent, and ask God to quicken the life in the idea as he sees fit...Then make a journal entry about your personal Easter egg. Consider the whole image without analyzing it. Writing will structure and clarify this tentative inner event. (If you wish, share the entry with a friend, or in your small group.) After fully developing your inner imagery, consider taking a next step in journaling, with the practical question that could make your exercise more than a fantasy:

What effort and resources would I need to commit in order to bring the egg fully into being in my life? Would the time and effort be worthwhile?

SCRIPTURE REFLECTION: HATCHING THE EASTER EGG

<u>The Gospel According to John</u> 5:19-30, especially verse 26: **As the Father has life in himself, so he has granted the Son also to have life in himself.**

The overall goal of much inner work is the recovery of the *true* self. Considered practically, this work must involve bringing to birth, and then helping to mature, a genuine identity. This true self is the authentic person whom God has created and is bringing fully into being. At each moment it is spiritually possible to be in accord with the deepest self. But often there is a break between the person we want to be or think we are (the self who talks back in the mirror), and the *real* self (how we feel and see ourselves in quiet moments when we are not performing for anyone's evaluation). When there is a break between the surface self, and the one we recognize as "the real me," our feelings get lost and life will seem shallow. Then the awareness of God or spiritual concerns is constricted.

Life need not be shallow! The human spirit, the place of divine contact and awareness, is the bottom of the soul: itself a precious inner world of consciousness and of largely unconscious thoughts, decisions and feelings. In our day, many have lost or have never found the path to the human spirit. The way is inward through the soul. This is a narrow path; but it is always open to those who seek with perseverance. At the entrance to the descending path within one must leave behind the assumption that what is seen and known externally is essentially all there is, or even, all that matters. Deep within is the womb of birth and rebirth, to expand the image a bit. It is like the inside of an imaginary egg. An egg must be quickened or it remains as it is. And at some point one must leave the comfortable shell. C.S. Lewis warned, "We are like eggs at present. And you cannot go on indefinitely being just an ordinary, decent egg. We must be hatched or go bad." The womb is a tomb, until Spirit touching spirit, brings life to the soul. And life breaks out.

In St. John, chapter 3, there is a dialogue between Jesus and Nicodemus, a man who has matured well in most every way. It seems likely that Nicodemus was an achieving man probably with a grown family and stable marriage. He kept the religious ways, even to the point of being a leader in his community. But he knew, and maybe had always known in the few moments before sleep that something of fundamental import was missing. Where the man wanted to feel assured, vigorous and fulfilled, there was an empty staleness, and the recurring concern: *Is this all there is?* And so he comes; cloaked in the night of this depression, Nicodemus seeks out Jesus, who is so vibrant that others are lifted just by being near him. Perhaps this teacher might point out a door just beyond awareness that opens onto a vision of what life might yet become. Jesus comes straight to the point. What is merely natural in the usual sense is not enough. Something of another order must come to birth before the splendor of true life can be recognized, much less lived. **I tell you the truth, unless a man is born from above (or again), he cannot see the kingdom of God (John**

3:3). Jesus speaks to him about this heavenly birth as of **water and the Spirit** (3:5). And the process, which will enable the new birth to take place, involves the **lifting up of the Son of Man** (3:14). Then whoever believes in him **shall not perish, but have eternal life** (3:16). Jesus has come to bring about a new birth into an enduring life, and thereby to transform our existence from the merely natural to a fuller, deeper quality of being. This is what accounts for the emptiness an otherwise achieving person like Nicodemus needs to acknowledge and confront honestly. To express this enlivening process is the purpose behind this fourth Gospel: **These words are written that you might believe that Jesus is the Christ, the Son of God, and that believing you may have life in his name** (20:30). St. John describes this life as both **abundant** (10:10) and **eternal** (3:16). Eugene Peterson paraphrases this: "**more and better life than you ever dreamed of.**"

No doubt both abundance and eternity are dimensions of the same thing. Christianity is not just another religion: it is this real (more than natural and ordinary) life. And Jesus is not just the messenger, but God's Word en-fleshed (The *Logos* is a divine attribute). Jesus alone can bring about the new birth – an inward or *spiritual* event of enormous consequence. His enlightening Spirit is like the flame on a candle; only the touch of fire brings light and warmth to an otherwise merely decorative object. Until the Spirit comes, one might paraphrase the concern of Nicodemus this way: *Where is life's fiery, passionate, inexhaustible depth?* Some people never ask this question; but those who seek persistently, find.

St. John proclaims the divine mystery, and proclaims the gift of a second birth in Holy Baptism, **born of water and the Spirit** (3:5). There are two sides to this, something we must do and something God alone can do. *Water* implies a down-to-earth recognition of need that brings us, like Nicodemus, to Jesus, and also the Church's acceptance and cleansing. *Spirit* points to the heavenly touch that quickens and beckons toward a fuller life. This is about the sacrament of Holy Baptism, both as a temporal event – the kind of thing one can record on video and remember in detail – and also as an inward experience that is more subtle and sometimes ignored, but is nonetheless the essence of the Christian mystery.

New birth is a gift freely offered. But like all true gifts it must be actually accepted and unwrapped, and then integrated into the other elements of our life. As we mature in Christian spirituality, birthing should continue and deepen, like a rosebush always making new buds. Journeying along the Christian path it may be tempting to ask: *Is this surprising experience, livelier than the last, really the new birth? I feel like I've been born-again again!* Perhaps it is enough to say that most birthing is unconscious for the one coming to birth, though a great effort for the mother and often for others as well. By the time one is aware of being alive, having been born, one has been through much formative experience, dimly aware. After all, the natural child is walking about and has developed language by the time it is aware it even exists. Anyone who can say, "*Hey mom!*" has surely been born. So it is with the spiritual person. Any person who calls out to the one Jesus calls **Abba, our Father in heaven** (Romans 8:15-16), and is living a life structured around Christ - those who say **Jesus is Lord** (1 Corinthians 12:3) - such a person has surely been **born of the Spirit** (John 3:8). Yet there is a continuous birthing; the old remains and is at times further transformed.

Let us now give attention to the eternal dimension of spiritual beginning; especially since on this level of experience, birthing may happen many times. Various moments along the way will partake of and fill out the moment of new birth, and cause us to see with fresh eyes what is going on with us. The dimensions of abundance and eternity are both part of the same fullness. You may be able to recall several rebirth experiences, usually preceded by a depressing darkness that led you to ask again: *Is this all there is?* In a sense, we are always coming to birth until, through physical death, the soul enters the heavenly life where time, as we know it, is no more.

JOURNALING EXERCISE

For a scriptural feast, in contrast to the more familiar Bible study snack, set aside several hours to read straight through the Gospel According to

John. Consider that this gospel is intended not to present facts of theology, not to *just tell the story* as a reporter would. It is designed with a precise focus. The writer wants to strengthen each person's (yours included) life-enhancing relationship with God, that you may be fully alive **now**. Read with this in mind. Stop from time to time and reflect; converse with the material, perhaps by writing notes in your journal. (Organize by chapter and verse for future reference.) Ask the Holy Spirit to enliven the text for you. When it seems relevant answer this question: *What do I hear God saying to me in this passage?*

Then later, as a second reflection, consider these personal questions: *What kind of life have I already experienced by believing in Jesus? Are there any specific memories that come to mind? Note and describe these: What do I think the Lord wants to bring to birth in me just now? Are cooperating and believing related? If so, what would I need to do to cooperate with this?*

You may want to share part of this second reflection with a mentor, friend or group that has done the same exercise privately. Covenant to pray for one another about this sharing. A good way for groups to do this is to conclude with an informal prayer, for the concerns expressed by the person on each one's right, with the expressed willingness to do this each day in the coming week. Begin the next session by sharing something new that may have taken place in the last few days. This kind of sharing process is likely to enrich your growth, bringing insights and energy that otherwise will be missed.

MEDITATION: THE WATER OF LIFE

(Someone reads the text below with quiet music of the ocean, or listens to the passage as presented on the accompanying CD.)

In the mind's eye, take a quiet walk along a familiar shore. What do you see around you...Touch something and notice its texture...Notice the light and the temperature, and the different odors in the gentle breeze as you continue to walk along....

Now take a moment to attend to your thoughts. Find inside the feeling of gratitude for the gift of life, and for the abundant and eternal life God is pouring into time right now -filling this moment full to overflowing from within... (Make a long pause.)

Now turn towards the sea. And as you walk slowly out into the shallow water, notice each step; and listen to the prayer of thanksgiving from the liturgy of Holy Baptism (The Book of Common Prayer, 1982, page 306):

"We thank you, almighty God, for the gift of water. Over it the Holy Spirit moved in the beginning of creation. Through it you lead the children of Israel out of their bondage in Egypt into the land of promise. In it your Son Jesus received the baptism of John and was anointed by the Holy Spirit as the Messiah, the Christ, to lead us, through his death and resurrection, from the bondage of sin into everlasting life..."

Continue to walk slowly out into the gradually deepening water:

"We thank you, Father, for the water of Baptism. In it we are buried with Christ in his death. By it we share in his resurrection. Through it we are reborn by the Holy Spirit. Therefore in joyful obedience to your Son, we bring into his fellowship those who come to him in faith, baptizing them in the Name of the Father and of the Son and of the Holy Spirit..."

Now you are up to your chin...now completely immersed....Feel the flowing sea grasses. Think of the warm, dark waters of the womb. ... Then pushing up, and breaking the surface, float on your back. Fully relaxing, feel the salty water and your body working together as you float easily.... And listen to the waters' lapping voice, praising the Creator:

(Psalm 24:1)
The earth is the Lord's and everything in it,
The world and all who live in it;
For he founded it upon the seas,
And established it upon the waters,

(Psalm 29:1-3)
Ascribe to the Lord, O mighty ones,
Ascribe to the Lord glory and strength,
Ascribe to the Lord the glory due his name.
Worship the Lord in the splendor of his holiness.
The voice of the Lord is over the waters;
The God of glory thunders,
The Lord thunders over the mighty waters.

(Verses 10-11)
The Lord sits enthroned over the flood;
The Lord is enthroned as King forever.
The Lord blesses his people with peace.

(Genesis 1:1-3)
In the beginning God created the heavens and the earth.
Now the earth was formless and empty.
Darkness was over the surface of the deep
And the Spirit of God was hovering over the waters…

The voice of the Lord is over the waters. …

(St. John 1:1-5)
In the beginning was the Word,
And the Word was with God, and the Word was God.
He was with God in the beginning,
Through him all things were made.

Without him nothing was made that has been made.
In him was life, and that life is enlightening everyone.
The light shines in the darkness, but the darkness has not understood it
Or overcome it....

The voice of the Lord is over the waters.

Now as you swim back to shore, notice your reaction to what you have experienced...

(Recorded music is *La cathedrale engloutie*, Preludes, Book 1. by Claude Debussy. Find this and an audio meditation on the accompanying CD.)

If this meditation is done in a group, it would be good to ask, "*What happened, and how do you feel about this?*" Listen without giving any advice. Make sure everyone has time to share. Someone may offer a concluding prayer of thanks, acknowledging the newness God is bringing to birth in each person's life.

CHAPTER TWO

THE WOMB & THE DIVINE CHILD
THE HEART'S DESIRE

THE RUSSIAN BOX

We wander like typical tourists through the narrow streets of the French Quarter, thinking there must be somewhere, in this maze of commerce and Creole cuisine, a shop filled with special treasures calling us to bring something home. We need a souvenir, lovely and useless, and at just the right price that says we have been here, something to dust over the years that will permanently fix memories of a really good time together. Holding hands like honeymooners we turn down yet another alley and notice a window display of painted boxes. The doorbell jingles. We saunter in and scan the goods. Yes, these things seem to be affordable, and they look even better up close. The shopkeeper, a woman with a hint of central European accent, describes the artist whose works fill much of the store. The painter is a young Russian woman, very traditional, trained in St. Petersburg, married to an American and living in suburban New Orleans. Her boxes are representative of a Russian folk art. A variety of decorations covered several simply constructed six inch square boxes lined in velvet. The wood is nothing special, probably available in local craft stores, but elegantly decorated. The bright flowers and dark figures on the boxes are precisely painted and interesting, each one a bit different. But only one of these fascinates me; it struck some deep chord. And so after many second thoughts like, *Do we really need this, another thing to carry around in an already cluttered life?* We retrace our steps and buy this icon-box (so called by me) because this piece alone has an exquisitely painted image of the virgin and child. The Madonna with hands raised in the ancient position of praise reveals her child within her womblike garments. The child Jesus confidently enthroned there, holds a rolled scroll in one hand, and looks out to meet our eyes. The other hand is raised forever in Eastern Christianity's conventional gesture of blessing. This is a classic Orthodox image, a visual theological statement, known as the Virgin of the Sign: so-called in reference to the sign of Immanuel, "God with us," given to King Ahaz by the prophet Isaiah. There is nothing surprising in this portrait. It is stylized and sends always the same message like a corporate logo, but this box is wonderfully painted, especially in the details of the faces. One never tires of gazing at it. There is a presence.[1]

[1]The "Virgin of the Sign" and several other line drawings in this book are from a book of traditional icon models printed in Russia before the Revolution. Such a cartoon would have been used by the painter of our box. These sketches, known to Russians as *prorisi*, are very old guides for painters, treasured in their own right for the process of creating authentic icons. For complete color versions of the illustrations please refer to the CD found inside the back cover. The images are all from Wikimedia Commons and may be found online in the Public Domain.

The painter knew what she was doing, and did it so well I wondered if the wooden lid was worthy of so much care, like painting a fine water-color on cheap paper. But then I remembered the finest old icons were painted on ordinary wood prepared according to particular rules. Inside the painted container are three wooden eggs, about the size of a robin's eggs. Each one is decorated differently. These I think must represent the Trinity or perhaps the Easter life of grace within the soul. I don't know for sure, but perhaps this inner content is traditional as well as the icon lid, in some cold corner of Russia.

For years we have kept this box in our home in a place by a staircase where we pass by it many times each day. Sometimes it reminds me of other containers with special meanings. Upstairs there is a stained wooden box I made early in our marriage to organize my wife's jewelry. It's rather clumsy; since I am not a craftsman. But she has kept it over the years, and filled it with colorful things that enhance the delicate tones of her pale skin. And I have a Cuban cigar box full of mementos, like the tooth fairy's collection of baby teeth. Its lid has a collage of glued shells, picked up carefully at low tide by our children on a trip to the shore. Some boxes would be hard to discard.

And allowing my thoughts to flow with images, I think of Long John Silver's treasure chest laden with Pieces of Eight, a magnetic box attracting rascals and heroes, a chest with hidden possibilities compelling enough to move the adventure from chapter to chapter through tropical foliage and unexpected detours. Then I think of the Ark of the Covenant, which one modern version translated as "covenant box" so children would not stumble over archaic vocabulary. (Then to movie theaters came the popular Raiders of the Lost Ark whose plot details our children knew more of than the Bible.) This box carried a spiritual power from both its function and contents. With it came a taboo so strong that for the wrong person at the wrong time to touch it meant certain death, like grabbing a fallen electrical line. But of course, the contents were what mattered and why such respect was given. The Ark contained the sacred mementos of God's covenant arrangement with his people. Mainly it included the Tablets of the Law divinely inscribed for Moses on Mt. Sinai.

Many special containers come to mind when I think of our Russian icon box. But sometimes I pause at its place on the table by the stairs, and let the imagined dark space within the Russian box be filled with my heart's treasures. What is most important to me just now? What are my cherished memories? What aspirations if realized would fill my emptiness? These are large questions; and they come up in bits and pieces, sometimes at inconvenient moments. But when these thoughts are done I rest my mind lightly upon the velvet-lined darkness within the box- a place left vacant, except for three small painted eggs, a place to have been and to become.

JOURNALING EXERCISE

As a prelude to journaling, consider what containers do. They hold things, separate things in an orderly way. Drawers provide a place for clothes that don't belong on the floor. Containers protect their contents, and provide a safe environment (food jars and refrigerators). They may allow us to move things from one place to another – like cars do. Some containers provide environments for transforming their contents under certain conditions - incubators and ovens for example. Our lives, too, are contained in many ways. Habits sort things out quickly in the mind. Childhood memories carve paths in the inner landscape and then like rains, tend to flow through the same paths carving even deeper channels. Our culture and family and religious heritages present us with containers. We may care for them like disposable paper cups, or like crystal goblets blazoned with a grandmother's monogram, or like the silver chalice the priest lifts from the altar, saying: "This cup is my blood".

The kinds of community we share also contain life. We settle down in community, which carries us along. It may or may not encourage growth, discovery and new adventure. Monastic life is structured to unite the community with God. The "institution" of marriage is constructed to contain an ongoing couple relationship. It is a traditional way to build the family nest so as to weather the changes of life over a long time.

Monasteries and family homes contain this life with architecture, but the institutions and cultures within them also are boxes of a sort, crafted to hold and nurture a certain process of life. Or they could be seen as vessels to store a precious liquid which may sometimes blend marvelously, picking up characteristics of the cask and gathering potency and value.

Sometimes we need to pay attention to the containers that form and enclose our lives, because they define and refine us, very often without conscious awareness.

Containers also confine the contents; there is a dark and light side to this process. Jesus said: **You cannot put new wine in old wineskins.** Surely there is truth here. But there is also truth in aging great wine in fine old French casks as long as conditions are right and leaks are well patched. Isaiah spoke of Mt. Zion, and many think of Calvary, when he prophesied: **On this mountain, the Lord of hosts will make for all peoples a feast of fat things, a feast of wine on the lees...wine on the lees well-refined** (Isaiah 25:6). Sometimes the container needs to be changed to suit the state of what is inside or the process that should be going on within; sometimes not. But one should be aware.

Here is an inner exercise to bring to mind some of the structures that shape your particular life. Reflection and discussion will follow. You may wish to listen to this script on the accompanying CD, or have some one present it in your group with quiet music. (Suggested: *Saturn,* from "The Planets" by Gustave Holst)

MEDITATION: THE WONDERFUL CUBE

Take a comfortable position in a quiet place. Become attentive and present by noticing with each sense what is happening around you in this environment...Then close your eyes. You may also want to notice each breath for a while... Relax and check your body for any tightness that needs to be released. Muscles usually relax if you tense a bit and gently relax this part. Most of us build tension in certain parts of the body- shoulders or lower back, maybe in the neck. Take note of this, and relax fully.

When you are ready, eyes still closed, gently slide through the quiet shadows inside, moving deeper within... Focus from time to time on your breathing to become completely present...(Pause)

You will see a large solid object, softly glowing up ahead, and drawing slowly closer. You can make out a sign with these words: A Place to Spend an Ideal Day. *Shortly you will enter this cube through the mind's eye and move through several enjoyable episodes.*

Enter now, and you will wake up in the bedroom, refreshed and ready to begin a wonderful day. During this day you may be anyplace at all and surrounded by the environment you wish in all its details. You will find yourself able to do whatever you want... Take a few moments just to be in this place; look around, you may go over and look out the window just to let the cobwebs go from your mind.

In a moment you will enter your morning room, where you will be wherever you would like to be and do whatever, taking as long a necessary. Allow yourself to enter and fully develop this experience starting now... LONG PAUSE

It's getting on towards mid-day. What did you find so pleasant about this? What memory would you like to carry along?...Now it's time to pass the afternoon in a different kind of activity; you can be anywhere and under any circumstances you wish, whether alone or with others. Just let this take place, right now...LONG PAUSE

Now find an impression or souvenir of this lovely afternoon to take along...It's been a long day and you're getting ready for an evening meal. This will be a place of refreshment. You can have this meal anywhere you wish, with whomever or alone, and take as long as you like... Enjoy dinner now... PAUSE

What made this meal so wonderful? Is there anything you might want to remember about it?...Now it is time to leave this inner place. Of course you can return in imagination from time to time, though things might be different... Now you're outside the luminous cube, floating once again in space, and when you're ready, gently return to the place where we began... aware of your breathing...aware of your body and of the space we share together. When you're ready, open your eyes.

Describe this inner journey in writing; or sketch it, if this is how your mind works. Only then consider further what the morning, afternoon and dinner experiences mean to you. Let each event explain itself. It may reveal layers of meaning.

Reflect on this question in writing, and/or by discussing it: What are the things that shape and contain my life? List and describe briefly.

What about this experience was fun and playful? Is there still a child in me that likes to play, needs to play? Is there increased energy when I consider these questions?

Does this inner exercise reveal anything about my values and desires, what is really important to me? What if anything is in the way of fulfilling these needs just now?

SCRIPTURE REFLECTION:
THE TREASURE WITHIN - THE HEART'S DESIRE

One of Jesus' most suggestive parables is just a few words: **The kingdom of heaven is like treasure hidden in a field. When a man found it, he hid it again, and then in his joy went and sold all he had and bought that field.** (Matthew 13:44).

Kingdom of heaven is a phrase characteristic of Matthew's gospel. ("Kingdom of **God**" as in Mark may have been Jesus' original term). In John there are other images to describe what Jesus comes to proclaim and make available. Here are terms such as *Spirit, Truth, Light-* and especially *Life, Abundant* and *Eternal*. These concepts are the core of Jesus' message according to John, as *kingdom of heaven* is for Matthew. And each evokes the ideal, the greatest blessing; which will always be partly found and partly hidden, as in the parable. We can be sure what Jesus proclaims and intends to give us is completely desirable and fulfilling, more enjoyable than the greatest physical pleasure. It is this promise of joy we tend to lose sight of. However, even a foretaste of this joy can make every hardship a learning experience, every moment of creation worthwhile. Jesus, we are told, faced even his rejection and tortured death, **for the joy that was set before him** (Hebrews 12:2). The parable of the hidden treasure is about the motivating power of joy. And Jesus' ultimate value **the kingdom of heaven** is all about the joy hidden among and within us. The heart of Jesus' proclamation was to assure us that there is joy, and though hidden, it is **at hand** (Matthew 4:17).

God has hidden this treasure nearby, in a place where we will eventually stumble upon it and exclaim in instant recognition: "This is it, what I have always hoped to discover!" The field is the deep heart of human experience. To find a field one must search the terrain. To find the spiritual "heart," look carefully within. What a tragedy to stumble upon something at hand and available without noticing its value. There was a man who took the worn Native American blanket from the back of his sofa to the "Antiques Road Show" for appraisal. He knew it might be worth something just due to age. How shocked he was to learn that he had been treating as ordinary the now priceless ceremonial robe of a great and famous Chief.

Beneath what matters to us are deeper values still. Jesus said, **Where your treasure is, there will your heart be also** (Matthew 6:21). Our treasure, always a cause for rejoicing, leads then to the heart, where the ultimate joy waits for us to discover it. When we recognize the deepest desires of the heart for what they really are, we will gladly do anything we must to make the field our own. There is always a problem with satisfying our longings – we don't own the field. Or as Jeremiah and nearly everyone since sadly noted: **The heart is deceitful above all things, and desperately corrupt; who can understand it?** (Jeremiah 17:9) Have you ever noticed how often people want something badly and do amazing things to assure it doesn't happen? And yet how difficult it is to recognize our own ways of "shooting ourselves in the foot" just as the race begins. We tend to prefer the familiar even when it perpetuates unhappiness. What's even more deceptive, we tend to prefer as Aristotle noticed, "the good", which is the enemy of "the better." Perhaps this is the gracious wisdom of our situation; having the treasure, yet not owning it, we may eventually come to want and even cherish what is best. Taking a clear look at the deep desires of the heart is difficult, but with patient attention to God's work deep within, we can bring to light the most satisfying treasure and make it our own.

The great spiritual teachers have recognized that the heart can stew in its desires, and it can be addicted to seeking what will cease to satisfy. Nevertheless at its deepest, the human heart longs for what is ultimately joyous satisfaction. A clear sign of this is desire itself. Stumbling upon the proclamation of **the kingdom of heaven**, one's desires begin to search out, and then uncover real joy. St. Augustine has expressed this in a classic saying: "Thou hast made us on the way to thee (or, "for thyself"); and our hearts are restless until they find their rest in thee." We must locate and follow the restless heart to its happy home. When we are at peace we know we are close to home. We begin to recognize what needs to be done to satisfy the soul. Further changes will become easier. Recognizing the truth, the truth liberates.

JOURNALING EXERCISE

Visualize with me the story (Luke 19:1-10) of Zacchaeus, a small man whose big heart knew what he was looking for. Luke mentions that Jesus was drawing near with his friends. His reputation went before him. Something of heaven was moving down toward Jericho in this wonderful person. Zacchaeus always felt it necessary to do a bit more than others to get ahead, sometimes at the cost of cheating on deals. So today the little guy was right in character to stand on someone else's donkey to boost himself up into the sycamore tree He wanted to see Jesus for himself; he had to compensate.

Lord, I too desire so much, help me like Zacchaeus to find what I really want, what is really worth living for.

So Zacchaeus waits in the sycamore. He holds onto the trunk for dear life, sitting on the bottom branch, spindly legs dangling in space. He feels the heat of the day, though leaves shelter him somewhat from the sun's rays. It's nearly noon and waves of heat rise with smells from the crowd now lining the dusty road into the city. He waits a while longer asking himself: *Why am I up this tree anyway? What do I really want?* Zacchaeus sits with restless heart, just wanting.

"I too Lord want so many things, hope for so much. Here I am, waiting with longing heart, looking for something or someone to come by and hold my attention. Help me to wait in the heat of the day for you to show up, Lord."

Jesus at last appears in the distance weaving through the throng reaching out to glimpse or touch him. But even for a small man, the sycamore is an insecure perch, the frail branch, bends and down slumps Zacchaeus upon the heads and shoulders of the others. Jesus notices: **Zacchaeus, make haste and come down; for I must stay at your house today.** With boundless joy, he scrambles down; the little man leads the way home. He bursts out in cascades of laughter and stammers exclamations, like a songbird whose moment has arrived.

"Lord whenever I sense your presence, I am surprised and all the best within me comes without hesitation to welcome you. Let praise and glory be yours forever."

The crowd grumbles, and a few call out some phrases about cheating in business. Zacchaeus is known to be a rascal. The little man is not defensive. He is sorry; he will repay. His concerns will be forever different. For now he has found the treasure, he will do immediately whatever it takes to make it his own. Today the King is coming home to dinner.

"Lord, heaven cannot contain you, nor can earth hold you, yet you come to my place and take up residence. Help me to find my heart's desire in you and to correct things done amiss along the way."

Journaling Question: What are the deepest desires of my heart? What is preventing me from finding satisfaction?

JOURNALING EXERCISE: THE ANNUNCIATION

Finally, consider the perfect container, Mary the mother of Jesus. She does not contain God as a box holds its contents. There is a more intimate and involved relationship. She gives him her genetic being, our human nature. He in turn has found a way to take our nature and to give us his divinity. She could not fully understand this, nor can we. Nor can we predict what it might mean for the future, hers or ours. But she could wait out her sense of vocation and focus her heart's desire, so that when the angel announced God's purpose to her, she knew they must be in one, **Let it be to me according to your word** (Luke 1:38). And then the thread of God's Spirit began to weave itself with new strength and clarity within human nature.

"The Annunciation to Mary"

Many of the classic icons of the "Annunciation to Mary" show her occupied with needlework. She holds, sometimes she drops in surprise, a skein of red thread. This image is an echo of Mary's childhood formation as contained in an apocryphal tradition. The young Mary's occupation was to weave a new scarlet curtain, the "veil" before the "Holy of Holies" in the Jerusalem Temple - a symbolic task with much resonance for the future. This process continues in everyone's spiritual life; for God is still weaving the red thread of his Spirit through the circumstances and opportunities of each day.

It is not just babies that require a womb, delivery and mothering. There must always be a container that makes it possible to receive gifts and to bring the heart's desires into concrete realization. That container needs to be available, suitable and prepared.

Some examples: To boil water one needs a pan and heat. But the really important matters are not always so obvious.

The desire to *give back* may need lots of research, training and planning to be effectively expressed, and to become more than a good impulse.

To stop drinking may require rehab and a life-time of AA meetings, plus that miraculous impulse to sobriety, another life altogether.

To *shape up* will involve gym membership, maybe a trainer, but also a firmly focused desire to make and remake changes in lifestyle.

To keep spirituality growing always requires considered religious practice to mature. The memory of a genuine conversion can only motivate for a while; and may even become a hindrance to developing faith by creating false expectations. As with form and content, container and contained are both important. Paul wrote: **We have this treasure in earthen vessels** (II Corinthians 4:7). But even clay pots can hold what is priceless. Of course a bejeweled urn may contain nothing but ashes and memories.

Journaling Question: *List all of your heart's desires from the previous questions, and also any new opportunities and happenings in your life. For each one, decide if you are truly willing and able to pursue it —to say, "Yes."*

*Then decide what **container** is available and suitable to protect the new life, and allow it to grow up.*

CHAPTER THREE

THE YOUTH
TRANSITION & ENGAGEMENT

THE RED THREAD

It was one of those rare days anywhere: "a clear day" when, as the song says, "you can see forever." The summits were all fogged in when she arrived at the base camp yesterday. She knew the great range was there, she didn't need to see it; but it would be nice to catch a glimpse, and here it was. Four AM, glistening in moonlight, shimmering with stars in the thin air, the smell of pines everywhere and no sound; she heard perfect stillness. The quiet seemed to have a life of its own, like the charged atmosphere before the music starts and where it goes after the last chord. It was good to get an early start. She was exhilarated with anticipation, and by what she saw, which made all this seem like more than her first solo climbing experience in the wilderness. She was all confidence, young and healthy, with the right gear. What did she have to fear but the unknown? Well, at her age, most of the time allotted to her life was yet unknown. And she hoped things weren't all planned out by some "moving finger having writ" type God. What if everything turns out to be planned and all the future is just like a walk through someone else's life? Bo-ring! After packing some more provisions and checking the rest of her stuff, she began the trail. She wanted to go alone; she figured it would be manageable if she stuck to the trail. Up is up, right? No real need for a compass, nowhere to go but uphill, foot by slogging foot towards the timberline and then to the summit. She certainly would have no trouble recognizing the peak. From the campground it had appeared so close that she had waved one hand before her eyes, checking the illusion that one might touch the glistening snow field and tap a finger on the summit's tip.

Now, of course only the trailhead was in view and the peak must be twenty miles as the crow flies, through the pines that drew her into the fragrant dark woods. She walked until the trail narrowed and finally seemed to end. Then she turned sharply uphill, climbing through a rock pile, something left by a glacier, no doubt. As she kept going up she thought: *Who needs a trail anyway?* She had instincts, woman's intuition as they say, and she knew what things should be like and what to avoid. By lunchtime she realized there was no trail to the top, not even a primitive one, and she couldn't really tell how far she had gone. Should she go on or go back? For the first time as she stopped to take out her lunch, the unknown seemed unnerving and the silence seemed cold and impersonal, not something to float songs on. She ruminated as she ate her tuna sandwich and laughed at comparing herself to a cow. She thought of the Native Americans (boys, at least; supposedly only they could become "braves.") who went off on vision quests to let nature's forces declare themselves, and find a sense of direction for their lives. But then she wasn't a boy, and for sure not a Sioux. How could, and why should, a Presbyterian go off on a vision quest? She knew someone was out there. These great mountains weren't just an accident, a freak collision of continental plates or whatever. And then there was music. The universe sang to her but, as the Gulf War period song had it: "From a distance, God is watching over us." Food and thin air made her drowsy. She nodded off for a few minutes and heard herself directing her thoughts: *God, if you really care enough to be here in person, show me the way. I'm lost.*

She woke up with a start, eyes caught by a red thread stuck on a rock.

This is spooky. It reminded her of Hansel's bread crumbs, and she shuddered. Sure enough, a bit farther along another wisp of the same bright red thread stood out among the gray stones. And then other bits, clearly placed with small stones preventing the wind or rain from carrying the bits of yarn away. Almost like those little streaks of colored paint they use to mark ski touring trails, but these were two-inch threads that lay near the ground. *Little red signs that God wants me to make it to the top*, she thought. *I'd better keep praying.* It was curious to consider that she was having a real religious experience, like the people in Medjugorie or something. But there it was, right in front of her eyes, actual thread forming a path of signs.

After about half an hour she realized there were not such simple answers for those who ask. The red-marked path, scarcely a trail, did not go up but gradually down, and it was getting late. No time left now to make it to the top, and she had wasted all afternoon unraveling a mirage, not a miracle. So much for prayer and red threads! As she turned to follow the fall line back, she caught a glimpse of more red, a bigger patch she couldn't ignore. Just behind a clump of bushes a girl about her age was sleeping, or maybe dead. Well, it turned out, she just had a bad sprain, nothing broken.

"I prayed a lot, more than I ever have, but got no answers," the girl said. "Then an idea struck me, a pretty silly one, but it's what occurred to me. So I unraveled my old red sweater a little at a time and tore off little pieces so maybe someone could find me. I started to crawl around and down the slope, leaving bits under rocks to make a trail. I stopped to eat and decided to spend the night because I was so tired and was glad I had packed my sleeping bag. Last night was cold for August, but clear with stars. I had time to think and pray. No scary wild creatures, except once something raced across my sleeping bag, probably a raccoon or something. Then sleep came, but no scary dreams. And then you showed up; you must be an angel or something. Please don't go without me."

It was well past dark when the two new friends stumbled exhausted back to camp, spent from leaning on each other and using three legs to move along. They became pretty good at it, and the sprain didn't hurt much as long as there was no direct pressure. Feeling a bit more grown up, both were wondering in different ways about the red thread God had knit into things.

JOURNAL EXERCISE: FINDING THE WAY UP

The successful transition to adulthood requires separation from parental voices who speak for us. Even small children fumbling with shoelaces will say, "I can do it by myself." Still, the task of being on one's own and capable requires many years of growth. Without skilful parenting, children struggle to succeed away from the family nest. We all know that families pass along strengths but also handicaps of many kinds. The little story about the Red Thread presents two lone climbers: two young women who are becoming whole, single individuals. They learn to rely on each other, like teams do, but remain solitary. Henri Nouwen in Reaching Out[2] says that the process of spiritual development involves a threefold movement: in relation to self, we must move from alienation to solitude; in relation to others, we move from hostility to hospitality; in relation to God, we move from illusion to reality. These three inner processes of spiritual movement are intertwined like strands of rope. The spiritual path at any moment will offer distinct contrasts for choices, like a woven pattern.

Nouwen's simple yet profound model is useful in many ways. It shows how intertwined our lives are with others, and that even within ourselves there is relationship, like the relationship within God the Trinity. All this is in motion: an ongoing flow. Stopping to examine ourselves at any point, we can grow when we make a positive decision about any of these three tendencies. It is not easy to take a sober look at each day's experiences, issues and choices and reflect on them, but such is the case with most spiritual consideration. It is necessary to stop all movement and really look and listen to the deepest places within for the truth of the situation. When this occurs and one responds with appropriate action, following Nouwen, then there is spiritual growth and a person is maturing.

Along this path, starting around puberty, a major change begins when one starts to make decisions as a single person. The experience of healthy solitude, "standing on one's own two feet" becomes of primary importance. This part of the journey of life is slippery and perilous. In modern western culture, the period of adolescence is quite long. In most of history, people married soon after puberty and the transition between one form of family life and another was rapid. This made things less troublesome in some ways. But this abbreviated youth happened at the cost of education, and there was minimal freedom of choice and restricted social mobility, especially for women. One of the interesting aspects of the lengthy western

---

[2]Nouwen, Henri, *Reaching Out: The Three Movements of the Spiritual Life,* Zondervan, 1998

adolescence is that "youth" can now have a separate identity, taking the shape of a long hiatus from maturity. This seems to be at bottom a spiritual issue. Perhaps the religious institutions we have inherited are problematic for many young people because they are associated too much with stability and parental voices representing external authority. There is within Christianity a point of contact with the adolescent, the person who deeply needs to differentiate self from other, to think independently, to find a new way to be and live.

Let us note that it is not only the physically young in our culture that are spiritually adolescent. The images of the aging rock star who is still engaging in the same things that teenagers do, and of Peter Pan who won't grow up, suggest a certain alienating tendency at the heart of western cultural experience. Christian spirituality can provide guidance and direction that minimizes the authoritarian parental voice and maximizes the movement toward peer support and healthy spiritual solitude. There is much complaining in the mass media of the demise of traditional values, but there is also unwillingness to celebrate the articulation of the wisdom of past ages.

Journaling Exercises: Make notes using Henri Nouwen's model of spiritual movement in your life.

How has my personal story been moving from alienation to solitude? Can I see God's involvement in this process?

Looking at my history of relationships, am I becoming less hostile and more hospitable over time? What is the evidence of this movement?

What experiences have shown a movement from illusion to reality in my relationship with God?

Is there a "red thread" weaving through my life's tapestry as I prayerfully remember my past? How does my

story and its apparent meaning change over the years as successive chapters are added?

The image on the next page is a partial pattern for an "Emmanuel" icon. In the tradition, such portraits may be of a beardless youth of varying ages

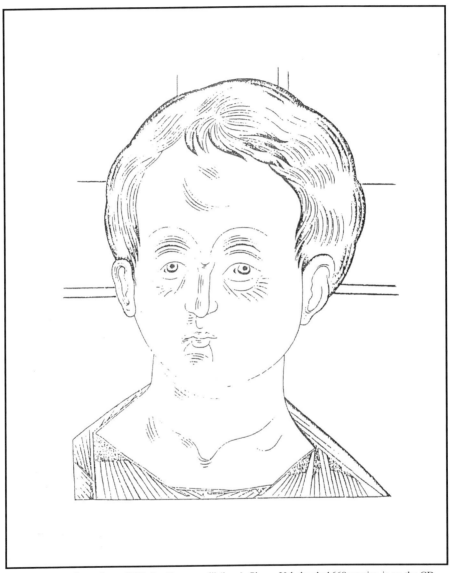

An old cartoon for an icon of "Christ, Emmanuel" (icon). Simon Ushakov's 1668 version is on the CD.

up to about twelve. Though the canonical scriptures do not speak of the formation of Jesus' self-awareness, the tradition asserts his embodiment of the divine wisdom even in this phase of development. One might appreciate the novel, Christ the Lord, by Anne Rice; it explores the dark period of Jesus pre-adolescent life with restraint, imagination and keen, theological awareness.

Scripture Reflection:
Identifying with Christ the Youth

In the canonical Gospels there is only one glimpse of Jesus as a maturing boy. This is early in the Gospel According to St. Luke. It may be the best source for pondering the spirituality of adolescence (whatever one's age). It is the story of a family journey: the holy family takes a trip to Jerusalem, an annual pilgrimage, but this time Jesus begins the process of separating from his earthly family and begins to move forward as a single young adult. Adolescence involves separation from parents and a family past and finding one's own identity, and moving along with inner motivation. The essence of this seems distilled in three moments sketched in Luke 2: 41-52.

1. **Now his parents went to Jerusalem every year at the feast of the Passover. And when he was twelve years old, they went up according to the custom; and when the feast was ending, as they were returning, the boy Jesus stayed behind in Jerusalem. His parents did not know it, but supposing him to be in the company they went a day's journey, and they sought him among their kinsfolk and acquaintances; and when they did not find him they returned to Jerusalem seeking him.**

This is about diverging paths in a family's behavioral expectation, and an individual's natural separation from it. The annual going up for the Passover from Nazareth to Jerusalem must have been like our family vacations. The children are packed, along with food and suitcases, in the old family vehicle. There are picnic breaks and potty stops, siblings and pets to deal with. The strengths and weaknesses of the family culture are revealed, its peculiar character and culture etched in the memory of the participants in such events. Take some time now to describe such a family trip from your own memories. Perhaps it is an annual trip to the country or holiday celebration that comes to mind. Picture yourself in this as a young teenager and recall the experience in as much detail as you can. After writing the story, consider these questions:

How did my parents handle letting me be on my own while still being part of the family?

Did I feel more secure or more confused as an adolescent, generally abandoned or encouraged by my family?

What trends, fashions, and attitudes shaped your journey through adolescence? How do these things still affect the way you live, think and pray? Is there anything I want to leave behind even now?

How did I go about separating from my parents and becoming my own person?

What are the areas within me that show I have not successfully finished moving into being a single adult as opposed to being a dependent child?

2. In the second scene (Luke 2:46-47) we arrive at a static moment. The boy Jesus has gone off somewhere on his own while the parents are frantic with worry, searching everywhere. They have run out into byways and side tracks, and return to where they last saw him. They brought Jesus once again to the Temple (as they had in infancy) and this time he has stayed there:

After three days they found him in the Temple, sitting among the teachers, listening to them and asking them questions; and all who heard him were amazed at his understanding and his answers.

This scene represents the archetypal moment of becoming adult, though astonishingly young. He has become his own person, no longer dependent upon others, and yet he is not alienated from his family. In returning to Nazareth, Jesus will be **obedient to his parents** (verse 51). Having defined the ultimate center of his authority in **his Father's house** he has chosen his duty. The traditional depiction of the story from the Eastern Church calls this moment to our attention: Jesus is in the center of the icon, revealing the divine within adolescence. This is the aspect of the divine which has been undervalued most in our time: the Lord of Transition, on the edge of adulthood. He is the opposite of the wild boys in William Golding's The Lord of the Flies, a story to which most adolescents can relate; they torment each other out of fear and self-doubt, instead of behaving as friends. Still there is also in late childhood a hidden divinity: the playful God who is our true Friend. The Christ in the Temple shows this other aspect of youth. The genuinely adolescent person is represented not as a child, not as an adult. It is this Christ which Christian teenagers have often found in their own community of peers: especially on youth-led retreats, I have seen this miraculous manifestation of Christ as Friend, where the young people have decided to put the needs of the retreatants first and do specific, loving and kind things for them, with intentional caring. This sort of behavior definitely reveals an encounter with Christ depicted in the icon - the divine older brother who knows the ropes and will show the way. The capacity for friendship with God is quite astonishing, but Jesus took this along into his permanent relationship with his disciples. (**From now on I call you friends** [John 15: 12-15].) Many persons have developed only a limited or blocked spiritual life because they have restricted their openness to God to relating to him only as Divine Parent. The approach to God as Divine Friend is essential to teenagers as well as to the adolescent within us all. We look inside for God as a Friend, Someone who is "by my side and on my side," not condoning all behavior, but benevolent and encouraging. Especially in times of transition and when we are seeking guidance, we need another Comforter. This presence is redemptive, and saves us from conforming to a lower standard of human behavior through peer pressure, and from the tragic consequences of sibling rivalry.

In your journal, consider your place in your family in relation to brothers and sisters and order of birth. Are you now able to relate to these family members as friends and not rivals? If not, why not? How have your siblings influenced you (and still do), and you them? (If you are an only child, how has this fact affected your capacity to be a friend to others?)

Write about three significant friends you have had in different periods in your life: childhood, adolescence, adulthood. Do your friends have things in common? Note how each friendship formed and developed. Consider how your experience of friendship and as a sibling has changed or developed over the years.

Is there anything you want to do to cultivate a current friendship or to bring closure to an old friendship?

Are there any ways in which a friend has represented God to you? How could you intentionally represent God in your friendships now?

3. Let us now consider the conclusion of the story of the 12-year-old Jesus in the Temple: the return journey. In the parent/child relationship, adolescence always brings in what was called in the 1960's "The Generation Gap"-often with moments or even years of painful, mutual misunderstanding. The Lucan story hints of this (Luke 2:48-52):

And when they saw him they were astonished; and his mother said to him, "Son why have you treated us so? Behold your father and I have been looking for you anxiously." And he said to them, "How is it that you sought me? Did you not know that I must be in my Father's house?" And they did not understand the saying which he spoke to them. And he went down with them and came to Nazareth, and was obedient to them; and his mother kept all these things in her heart.

And Jesus increased in wisdom and stature (or years), and in favor with God and man.

There is a 14th Century Italian painting by Simone Martini which at first looks very pious, much gold leaf and conventional portraiture, but the gestures wonderfully portray the recognizable dynamics of family life with an adolescent. The misunderstanding is all there: Mary is questioning her son (How often we wonder at the ways of God.), but she holds a book, surely a symbol of inspiration to search out the meaning of things and to treasure the questions. The young Jesus reminds us of a typical kid thinking, "Oh Mom, you'll just never get it!" The Christ who is usually shown with an open book and hand raised in blessing now has his arms folded on a closed book. Joseph reveals the pain of this conflict in his eyes and inclined head, attempting to bridge the gap between mother and son. Yet all this conflict is blessed with haloes and dazzling colors and the gold touches,

60

symbolic of Divine Glory. Doesn't this bring a hopeful aspect to family life? We don't always agree, and may never fully understand the other's viewpoint, yet this is part of a holy moment. Ambiguity and misunderstanding are part of the journey into and with the Divine, especially in phases of transition. God, at such moments, may be apprehended in the depths of the heart as friend, even peer.

Perhaps we should use a more traditional image for our meditation. Classic Eastern interpretations would never allow the personalizing touches we read into Simone Martini's Renaissance version; though Jesus is not portrayed literally by the boy next door as yet more modern painters might

"Christ Among the Elders", a pattern for iconographers

ПРЄПОЛОВЄНİЄ ИЛИ 12ᵀᴴ ЛѢТНİЙ ĪC.XР̄. ВО ХРАМѢ

do. The anonymous icon pattern reproduced here (and in color on the CD) focuses on the Temple scene; the beardless, twelve year old *Emmanuel* is enthroned among the elders; Joseph and Mary with somewhat neutral gestures, enter from the right. That there is little personal interpretation may set us free to encounter the central event and experience our individual responses which will change from time to time.

MEDITATION:
AN ENCOUNTER WITH CHRIST THE YOUTH

This inner exercise could be done alone or as the second part of a group session. Work through some of the earlier material in this chapter; and then go through each of the three parts with brief sharing on what happened. Listen to each other carefully, but without critical comment. The intent is to bring each part to fullness of apprehension. The sections deepen and should be presented in order after a period of centering and quiet. (The meditation with music is on the CD.)

Quietly take an imaginary journey into the scene of the adolescent Christ in the Temple at Jerusalem, sensing the surroundings and atmosphere...

1. Now focus on Jesus amidst the teachers, listening, questioning. What is the subject for discussion, and what are they saying about it? Let this happen easily, as though you were watching a movie...

2. Now let yourself be a young person. Experience your fantasy about what Jesus has been doing and what is beneath his response to his parents upon being found: "Did you not know I must be about my Father's business?" What might that mean for him?...

3. Next scene. Jesus beckons to your youthful "self" and seems so friendly that you are immediately at ease. You will be able to duck into an alcove with him for some time alone. Let a short conversation with the young Jesus take place in your imagination. ...

Conclude with conversational, verbal prayer expressing your response to this encounter.

Share what took place with this experience in the imagination. What really stood out? What do you think it means for your life? Listen for the uniqueness of others in your group. What did they experience? (If you are doing this alone. use your journal to reflect on the questions.)

CHAPTER FOUR

THE YOUNG ADULT
MASKS & TESTING

THE MASK

In the dim past, when the sages were speaking of deep matters, and the insides and outsides of things were perfect mirrors, there lived a scoundrel. This man was ugly in heart and visage, like a swamp toad; but he was clever, especially at crafts. In the same province lived a magnificent princess who swore to share her bed and inheritance only with the most worthy prince. This person was to present himself in accordance with the Emperor's edict: "Men of the realm give heed. All who desire the hand of the princess Ming Li should come forward for testing. All may try, but those she de-selects will also lose their heads; only the most handsome and virtuous will succeed."

The crafty scoundrel mulled over this opportunity and decided to risk all. He exercised much skill and effort to fashion a masterpiece – a "Handsome Prince" mask. This would conceal his homely face and his scummy heart. These were days when it was thought that finely wrought features with well-placed eyes and nose revealed the dignity and splendid character of a man.

Admiring the museum quality and perfect fit of his mask, the scoundrel believed himself prepared to travel to the imperial city to try out for *prince*. The princess, thoroughly deceived, chose the somewhat less than heroic craftsman over the unfortunate others. And with great festivities, they were pronounced "Prince & Princess." The crafty scoundrel knew how he must behave to play his part, and with Herculean effort he succeeded in living the good life. Eventually he grew weary of this pretense. Or perhaps a noble conscience started to develop within him. More and more he was tormented by not measuring up to the adulation of his bride. And so, one evening after an especially fine wine, he broke down in bitter tears. Thinking death better than this deception, he confessed the truth. The shocked princess could not fully accept this troubling revelation; and so she said, "If you are not my beloved, unmask yourself and let me see!" The scoundrel carefully peeled away the segments and layers of his elaborate artifice, and stood before her with downcast eyes. Only when she brought a mirror could he accept the truth. After such long and careful adjustment, he had become the role. The scoundrel was now totally a prince; and the two lived, of course, practically forever in heavenly bliss.

MANIFESTING THE TRUE SELF

"Who am I?" is always a good question. The answer is either obvious, and the question is tossed off; or it is unsettling, calling for serious reflection. The sense of identity is not stable. Physical changes shape our evolving sense of self in youth. And experiences reshape us. Yet there is a core of continuity throughout life. It would be interesting to chart how the sense of "who I am" has changed with biological development, shifting circumstances and events, and one's interpretation of these things. We might consider this shifting awareness as an up and down point moving through time as in this diagram:

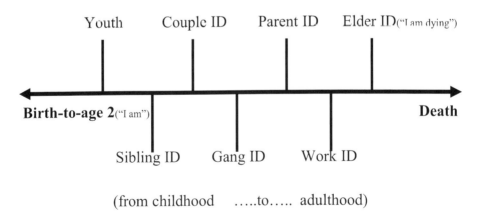

(from childhood   .....to..... adulthood)

The developing sense of identity can seem purely natural, but there is another dynamic; the deeper realm of self-awareness is archetypal and spiritual. Let us think of this non-temporal movement as a spiraling overlay to the straight-line diagram. The archetypal phases are accessible at many points along the periodic cycle of spirit and eternity:

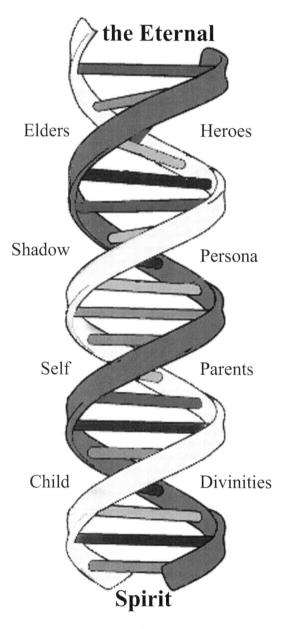

the Eternal

Elders   Heroes

Shadow   Persona

Self   Parents

Child   Divinities

Spirit

To become conscious of the spiritual dimension requires a deeper awakening and attention to dreams and other types of consciousness frequently unexplored or discounted. The *True Self* is part of all these elements, temporal and spiritual, and may be brought to awakening as in familiar folk tales, such as the Greek stories of Psyche and others. Religion and mythic stories provide surface access to these larger dimensions of self-awareness. Journaling and prayer will assist in the exploration.

St. Paul speaks of the spiritual dimension for Christians in several places; but especially in his awareness that **It is no longer I who live, but Christ who lives in me** (Galatians 2:20). Both this "not I" and "Christ within" are states of awareness generally available to adults and even to some children.

First of all, there is a wide range of experience early on of identity between "me-at-my-best" and "me-at-my-worst." And the developing conscience has a character with which most people can have inner conversation. This is probably the earliest awareness of a complex self which is helped or skewed by parenting. ("Listen to your conscience, my dear.") Then as the child develops and learns to adapt, there is a conventional character who takes shape, with perhaps several roles to play. These are sometimes called the *persona*, an archetypal manifestation that is usually the *self* one recognizes in daily dreams. (The "dreaming self" is of course different from the *self* one dreams about. In a later chapter we will consider a way to work with these and other archetypal manifestations as they appear in dreams.) After puberty, much masking becomes conscious, as we strive to fit in and be interesting to others as workers, friends and sexual persons. In youth we become actors, and we usually begin to feel and conceive life as though we *were* these masks, feeling alienated from the children we thought we once were, and wondering if the adult person will ever take shape. In between, we are student, girl-friend, soccer player, etc. The character gradually fills out. Still there is always a sense of core being, a continuous *self* that vaguely constitutes the answer to: "Who am I, anyway?"

When the rich inner and outer components of identity are not integrated, painful problems arise. This integration requires much effort, which is frequently neglected. For this reason, identity crises can develop all along life's path. These can manifest as "double-mindedness," or conflicts about how to behave appropriately, or vulnerability to substance abuse, etc. Sometimes a person feels painfully confused, with several centers of being – thinking, feeling and acting in conflicting ways. To explore, to sort out and integrate all these roles becomes a truly trying task with mythic perils, like the labors of Hercules. These issues can be amplified by such new roles as spouse and parent by this time. How, then, does an adult discern and live the *True Self*? Is there a way to help us live authentic and integrated lives in tune with our deepest aspirations and values?

THE MATTER OF CONSCIENCE

The faculty of human conscience is not often considered these days; but it should be. So let us digress. There is something in our everyday awareness which is sensitive to guilt: we have short-term twinges, and more enduring burdens of conscience. Psychoanalytic theory posits an inner mechanism to regulate behavior –the *super-ego*. Whatever we mean by the word, the conscience is not inborn. It begins to develop in toddlers along with language. The very young gradually internalize external regulations. Without admonition they would play in traffic, and drown the cat in the bathtub. And so, "*NO*" is a primary word with its familiar but shadowy associate, the sense of shame. As time moves on, guilt is also experienced when one is not good enough: not finishing homework, for example, or anxiety about being naughty when Santa is coming. The conscience continues to expand as authority figures amplify parental expectations. And groups we identify with also have norms spoken or veiled that impinge on conscience. Misunderstanding and complications thrive in the gloomy recesses of shame.

There are some, especially those with heavy-handed religious training, who feel guilty just in existing; like the characters in a Kafka novel, they seem to be "guilty of guilt." To the other extreme, prisons are full of sometimes charming persons who can hurt others without remorse, sociopaths. Between these extremes, most of us regulate daily behavior, and also cope with the sense of guilt and its attendant characters, remorse and shame; and of course, we often experience the essential mechanism of absolution. Forgiveness of self and others are both grounded in God's redemptive love. (For this reason one should usually consider three questions in order to clear the conscience: *Am I willing to let this go? Have I asked the other's forgiveness and made restitution? Have I prayed about it?*)

With care, the conscience can be reshaped and further matured by healthy religious convictions and effective spiritual practice. In the Bible the word appears without definition, but with adjectives that offer some insights. According to the New Testament, the conscience may be: **clear towards God and man** (as in Acts 24:11and I Peter 3:16); it may be **weakened and defiled** (I Corinthians 8:7); it may be **seared** (I Timothy 4:2), **pure** (Hebrews 9:14), or **perfect** (Hebrews 9:9).

The classical Christian approach to developing and maintaining a healthy conscience has much to commend it. Two practices are involved, self-examination and spiritual counsel:

Self-examination is subjective, but with an external standard. One might use the "Ten Commandments" explained and expanded by moral theologians; for example, note the Catechism of The Book of Common Prayer, 1982, pages 847-848. Expanded outlines of the "Seven Deadly Sins," are also widely used, as is the type of searching, personal inventory practiced in *12 Step* programs.

Self-examination alone is certain to be inadequate. We overlook major issues; and often feel guilty, though we are not guilty. For centuries one of the main roles of the cleric has been to serve as *confessor*. Sacramental confession with a discreet, trained, probably ordained spiritual director is different from most counseling but related. Its core function is what the English tradition has accurately called the "cure of souls." An occasional appointment for confession, usually with one's pastor or spiritual director, is of inestimable value to spiritual well-being and general health. (Note, James 5:14-16.)

Volumes have been written on each of these two practices, mostly read by the clergy; both self-examination and confession are actually quite simple, helpful and readily available to all. To neglect them is perilous, like driving your car without regular oil changes.

+++++++++++

The world's major religious traditions all provide ways to ground and develop the authentic personality. In fact, the word "religion" points to this; it comes from the Latin *religere*, which means "to bind back," as a *ligament* binds muscle to bone. Psychologically, religion functions like a hand grasping the strings of a set of brightly colored balloons. In this way our spirituality should hold the integrated *Self* as it matures, giving one room to discover and experiment yet within healthy limits. The practice of Christianity has a distinctive way of unifying and redeeming the whole personality by conforming it to Christ, the image of God. In the following imaginative exercises you are invited to explore conscious identity as an adult. Journal first; and only then, perhaps, share parts of this material with others. One should be especially careful about not sharing the details of confessional material.

JOURNALING: EXERCISES IN SELF DISCOVERY

1. In your memory, sort through several experiences of *guilt*; select two from childhood, two from young adulthood, and two others. Explore the ways in which you got into these situations and how you resolved them. Then see if you can detect any patterns of behavior in your journey of dealing with the crises between your "good self" and "bad self."

2. If you could paint a picture that revealed your *true* inner personality, what would you be doing? How would you be dressed? How would you be posed? At what age? Would you be carrying or holding something? What

71

about the background and choice of colors? Take a few minutes to become quiet, and then let your imagination portray yourself walking through an art gallery. Find your picture and let it take full shape in your mind's eye. What feeling comes up within you as you look at this portrait? What is the main feeling expressed in the painting itself? Be open to whatever this experience might mean to you right now.

3. Journey inside using your imagination. Relax, let your *conscience* take some specific form and personify it by giving it a voice. Have a conversation with your conscience in your journal, your own version of Jiminy Cricket and Pinocchio. (This could be an ongoing exercise.)

4. Exploring the masks and what may be behind them:

- If you could choose a suitable role for yourself in a play (any play), what would it be? How would the scene move along? In your imagination, let it happen, going along with the character.

- In your teens, what behavior did you admire in others of the same sex? What did you want to be like and how did you try to make that happen? How did you think others saw you and what did you do about that?

- In your family, was there a habitual function that you performed, whether or not you wanted to? Did this behavior feel natural, a part of yourself? If it is difficult to find and describe this, you may find one of these two questions helpful in writing a description:

  • In a crisis, members of my family seemed to just know what their place was and what to do. My role was _____?

  • My family had nicknames that helped define our characters. Mine was _____?

THE TESTING

I don't know if I can continue with all this. Those guys are all bigger than I am; and further, "kicking butt" is not my goal. She paced around gathering her karate gear. She stuffed her kicks and other blow-deflecting padding into her red duffle. She recognized this desire to withdraw; it was the downside of weeks of pushing herself to do more of everything, to be ready for the testing. It gets harder as the levels advance. The yellow belt was just another Saturday morning with the other kids. The brown belt took more preparation, about a year. Now she might be going to tournaments as a black belt where the competition was stiffer, and you felt silly to make a mistake in a *kata*. These formal exercises are cumulative for testing; now she knew about a dozen. They were hard to keep straight, except for that odd *kata* where you tighten all your muscles and slowly hiss. She still needed to slow this one down, and overcome her fear. She knew all the boys in the dojo would try to kick or punch at just the moment she'd be vulnerable and break her concentration. Her mom said the hissing breath seemed like those Lamaze exercises you learn for delivering a baby: to focus attention on the breathing so as not to feel the pain. She knew it could be done, but not without training. She just couldn't find the motivation to train. What would Sensei bark? "Get focused kid." So she sat back on her heels, pretended to be from Okinawa, and turned inward.

She thought about the poor islanders whose only weapons against invading warlords were farm implements. The Okinawans were not warriors by nature; but they had to find a way, a creative new way of self-defense, or be subjugated by feudal invaders interested in taking a big share of their crops. She began to remember her "advantage," as Sensei put it. She was the only girl in the dojo right now. There was another girl until recently; but she quit when her weight problem got under control. It certainly was not an advantage to be female; over the years the boys had all gotten bigger. She couldn't really remember drubbing one of them in sparring since the sixth grade – well, maybe if clumsy Eddie was having a bad day. No, she had learned to find advantages unique to being herself.

First, she wasn't a natural like Sensei and some others. Her body didn't think for her or train easily. She became a strategist; this kept it all from becoming so boring with repetition. There was always something to improve, a little adjustment this way or that. She also had the advantage of being like the Okinawans, vulnerable and shrewd. She learned as the boys grew and used their arrogant bravado, she would have to find strength in more than muscles; and she would have to turn negatives into assets. It was not easy, but she had become good, really good, at what more talented people took for granted. She did this by turning discouragement into challenge. So she sat there quietly on the edge of the mat thinking about all this. Still she could not find it in herself to train today. All her thoughts now seemed like excuses to quit. After all there are many paths to accomplishment in life.

And then the temptations set in like a winter storm. She could just quit. That's what she felt like doing right now; she could use a vacation from this daily routine. Lots of people quit. Over the years many other girls and boys had gotten bored or interested in other things. They could always come back to training, though no one ever did. She recognized this *"Let's quit"* thought and rebuked it almost out loud. Karate is one good way, if you stick to it, of getting control of yourself. If she had been the type to follow her feelings, she would have quit long ago. In this case, discipline was its own reward. There had to be a good reason to quit. Then the fears and doubts came up. The critical voices punched in: "This has all been a big waste." "You'll never be good enough to get a black belt." Her stomach tightened: *Just look at this assortment of reasons to fear karate: being hit, looking foolish, and forgetting everything, on and on and on.* For a few minutes she listened to these voices; then the storm subsided. She'd been to the place of illusions before, and let this go. The Zen masters taught how to deal with such thoughts; watch them drift by like boats on a river, just don't climb aboard.

Then she had a powerful idea. She could envision another dojo for girls only. Then she wouldn't have to work so hard, in fact they might even offer her a job working with the white belts on Saturdays. The girls there would think she was so cool, a real winner. Maybe this would even make her more popular at school, even with the boys, not that she really cared. This fantasy was really appealing, much more so than the black belt testing Sensei had scheduled for her next month. After maybe ten minutes excursion into this plan, a voice broke into the reverie; really it was just a word, "Pray." And then she asked for help and guidance, and listened. The memory of her first few weeks at the dojo came to mind. She was in the third grade. Her dad thought she was only in this for the crisp white *gi* that came with the month's trial offer. After the newness wore off, he figured, she would add the karate uniform to her dress-up collection, alongside her cowgirl outfit and the astronaut suit. But this had been an interest she constantly pursued for six years.

She had always been proud to be part of Sensei's dojo; he was a purist and believed in the value of karate. It had kept him going through those years when his parents split. This man was a champion kick-boxer, though she thought those days were over because of his broken bones, and being unwilling to come in second place. With his wife and their new baby, his interests were broadening. Thinking this way brought new energy and focus. Yes, for her karate was not just something to do. It was part of her very being since childhood; the part that would continue to develop. She needed to be true to who she was, and to who she was becoming. Now she was right on; end of attitude readjustment. She sprang up like a playful kitten, twirled around, and exploded into a nice kick to the head. "Ouss," she shrieked. "I can't wait to break a few boards, and kick some butt!"

SCRIPTURE REFLECTION:
THE THREE TEMPTATIONS OF CHRIST, AND THE CHRISTIAN

"The Three Temptations' (mosaic icon), San Marco, Venice, 12th Century

At his Baptism by John in the Jordan River, after the Father's voice confirmed Jesus' identity and purpose in life. **Immediately**, Mark wrote succinctly, **the Spirit drove him out into the wilderness to be tempted. He was in the wilderness forty days tempted by Satan. And he was with the wild beasts, and angels ministered to him** (Mark 1:12-13). The point is that though the enemy tests, it is a struggle inspired by God and it is required to manifest identity and purpose. For Jesus the testing by Satan must have ended in even firmer resolve to carve out a straight and narrow path leading to self-sacrifice instead of self-glorification.

Father Andrew sheds a bright light on the contest of Christ and the enemy in a letter to one of his spiritual correspondents dated December 24, 1945:[3]

In every experience of life God is with us, and if we abide in union with Him, the issue of the experience, <u>whatever it is</u>, will be God's glory, our sanctification, and the power to help others.

You can imagine the devil saying to our Lord, "You think you will save the world. You will come to our nation and they will excommunicate you. You will come to the common people; they will hear you as long as they can get something out of you; then they will hound you to death. You will collect around you a group of people, whom you will call your church, but they will just quarrel amongst themselves as to which is the greatest, and one of <u>them</u> will betray you, and one of <u>them</u> will deny you, and all will fail you, and your end will be defeat on a gallows, dying in the dark." Well, the devil was marvelously accurate. All he said would happen, did happen, but just because our Lord remained in union with the Father in it all, <u>those things</u> all became the very best possible way in which He did what He came to do; if the devil had set out to help Him instead of hinder Him, he could not have provided Him with a more perfect instrument for offering the sacrifice, revealing the Divine Character, and setting a perfect human example---the three

[3]Kathleen E Burne, *The Life and Letters of Father Andrew, S.D.C.*, Mowbray & Co., London, 1948

things He came to do---than the Cross. So the devil completely defeated himself, and <u>his</u> trump card, the Cross, became our Lord's trump card!

Mark has only two sentences. But Matthew and Luke provide content for three specific temptations. Just as the mythic Hercules' heroism was tested by difficult and strenuous labors, the heroic Christ faced tests that on failing would have derailed his mission and discredited his identity as Divine Son. Spiritual beings are always tested. Christians, sharing Jesus' being and purpose, will always face the same temptations:

1. Jesus was naturally famished after his long fast. When tempted to turn stones into bread he quoted scripture that affirmed: **Man shall not live by bread alone, but by every word that proceeds from the mouth of God** (Deuteronomy 8:3). We are not to be motivated by merely natural needs and tendencies. The Spirit-led life is focused on higher things. The tag word for this renunciation by all who come to Christian baptism is *the Flesh*; this involves putting the merely natural in the back seat. In this way the merely natural ("fleshly") can be redeemed by our spiritual nature.

2. Jesus was also tempted to establish a political kingdom, a path others encouraged him to take even to the last week of his life. One imagines a world-dominating vision like that offered by Satan in the Dore etching. But Jesus' mission was to be other than a local leader of Zealot liberators; he was not to be an imperial politician engaged with the Roman system; certainly he would not be cast in the role of world-conquering warrior like Alexander the Great had been. His vision was far broader in every dimension, not "worldly" at all. Christians, too, are called to be motivated by that which is beyond earthly prospect. By renouncing *the World*, the Christian's vow is not an escape or denial of the world and its problems. It is meant to be a vow that stands for refusing to be motivated like consumerist donkeys by the carrot always dangled before us by earth's movers and shakers. We should only be motivated by commitment to inward values and objectives, not by external motivation and the trade-offs with integrity that are always offered by "the prince of this world."

3. The triple renunciation of evil involves turning also from the voice of our personal enemy, that is, the Tempter. We are not likely to meet Satan in the guise of Halloween costumes or horror movies, but there is a voice and presence of evil sometimes touching us through that part of the archetype known as "The Shadow." Regularly, we are tempted to act on lies and fantasy; and Satan's most powerful motivator is fear. Jesus' test in this regard was to leap from the highest point of the Jerusalem Temple like a Hollywood stuntman, to force a divine intervention in his behalf. Had this happened and been successful, the whole process of selfless demonstration of divine power we know as Jesus' ministry of compassionate teaching and healing would have been side-tracked into a sideshow routine. Time and history could not be redeemed apart from the vulnerability of immersion in the murky waters of human nature. Jesus' victory over evil incorporates all who identify themselves with him; just as an earthly general's victory has consequences for all whom he represents.

Following the Spirit is only possible when we are continually loosed from the power known in old-fashioned theological shorthand as the *motivation of the flesh, the world, and the devil.* Jesus is the one who has, in fact, freed us from enslavement to evil powers. He has given us the freedom to renounce bondage and stand with him, motivated by the same Spirit that generated his coming fully into this world and then rising above it. From now on, the motivation of evil may always be recognized by ordinary awareness, and then renounced. Simple self-reflection is enough with God's help, to discover and then to turn away from these negative tendencies in order to be led positively by the power of the Spirit. This testing is a daily experience that must be incorporated into the Christian's normal spiritual practice. The teenage girl in the karate story faced and overcame each of these three spiritual enemies, just as we all can overcome daily in a more or less heroic struggle. The following reflections will suggest ways to be victorious in the contest with personal evil.

JOURNALING EXERCISE: UNPLUGGING FLESH, WORLD & DEVIL; THE SPIRIT - PLUGGING IN

1. Renouncing the Flesh. When the karate student in the story was dispirited and felt like quitting, she was experiencing the temptation of the flesh. St. Paul, especially in Galatians 5:16-25, lays out the classic distinction of the flesh/spirit contest. Read over this if it is not familiar. He seems to indicate there is a range of behavior always available; human nature has a "lower" and "higher" dimension. Left to inertia, the lower tendencies will usually win out.

Journaling Question: *When have I experienced recently the inner testing of the flesh? What have I done about this, and what were the consequences? Is there a fleshly tendency to which I am susceptible, a frequent pattern of suggestion? Journal about two or three past instances of testing in this area, considering much can be learned from failure as well as success.*

2. Renouncing the World. The karate student's strongest temptation was to abandon her deeply committed next step in favor of possible peer recognition, external motivation. She had a fantasy of "grass is greener on the other side." In so doing, her life would have been cut off from her renewable source of deep inner energy. An antidote to worldliness would be to ask, "Where is God involved in this situation?" And, "What is the ultimate value of this course of action?"

Journaling Question: *Identify an unsettled issue in your life that seems to be calling for your attention and consideration? How could this issue be addressed through a worldly approach? A spiritual approach? What difference would it make which choice you make?*

3. Renouncing Satan. The karate student successfully confronted the power of deception by refusing to listen to intimidating voices like, "You couldn't possibly succeed at this." The best way to confront such voices is with sober, continuous vigilance, and an objective dose of the truth – that is, by listening to someone whose opinion you respect. For many of us fear, deception and lies have been a constant source of inner attack. With regard

to the enemy, scripture says at different places, we should **rebuke, flee,** or **resist** when attacked. But we should never enter into dialogue with any person or being whose intent and mission is to deceive.

Journaling Question: *Make a journal entry about your history of contest with deception? Is there a pattern of fears that you have had to battle over the years? How have you heard the voice of self-doubt recently? What did you do in this case?*

4. <u>Motivation of the Spirit.</u> The issue of motivation comes up daily. The word *spirit* is a metaphor for wind and breath, the life energy that is basic for us. This is "the Force" in popular cinema mythology that is "with us." In Chinese philosophy it is *Chi.* Since spirit has a transcendent aspect it can be the personal manifestation of a particular deity. For Christians, God's Holy Spirit and the human spirit can be united in a relationship of love. Jesus taught that we should be confident about God's desire to give the Holy Spirit to us and to trust his goodness. With regard to the Spirit, he says: **Ask, and you will receive; seek, and you will find; knock, and the door will opened to you** (Matthew 7:7). By asking persistently and confidently for the Holy Spirit we are cleansed, inspired, renewed and motivated by God. In all four gospels Jesus is portrayed as the one who **baptizes with the Holy Spirit**. This must be a basic experience at the heart of our spiritual journey.

Journaling Question: *What has been your personal experience of God as Holy Spirit? If you have not been accustomed to regularly asking, seeking, knocking; consider doing this in a way that seems natural to you as you begin each day's activities.*

TWO MEDITATIONS ON CHRIST THE HERO

Both of these exercises are imaginative, but the first recollects images produced by artists in the great flow of Christian tradition. The second relies on the spontaneous generation of an image within the meditating person:

1. The Church over the centuries has pictured Christ in various ways,

all of which seem to point to the revelation of God in a specific human person. The doctrine of the incarnation justifies, even encourages such visual representation, which is forbidden by Jews and Muslims. (In history, the "Iconoclastic Controversy" gave thinkers the chance to give clear boundaries for Christian art and devotion. Those concerned about this can easily research it through books or articles on *iconoclasm*.) Perhaps you have accepted an image of Jesus as real and reliable. This could be an ancient icon you have used for meditation. It could be a picture that has been important to you since childhood. A great painter or sculptor may have made Christ meaningful and alive to you through a work of art. You may have it framed, or even as a bookmark in your Bible. You may have gone to a church with a stained glass window of Christ; you will remember how the light touched it in different ways over the years. The point is, though the historic person Jesus was not photographed, portrayed or even described physically in words, he was known, recognized and touched by many people. The faithful have always been drawn to certain images that seem to represent the Lord to the eyes of devotion. If you were to suddenly appear to a friend whom you had known only through phone calls or the internet; it would make no sense for your friend to say, "You are not your real self, because I thought you looked this way or that." Since the Ascension, Jesus has often appeared among us in recognizable visionary experience. There is likely to be enough agreement about the corporeality of Jesus to make him recognizable as the same person for his original disciples as he has been for those who have since known him spiritually. With this in mind, choose a representation of Jesus from the Christian church that is acceptable to you. This could be a Coptic icon, or a work from the Italian Renaissance, a Church School poster or a modern painting. Whatever comes to mind is probably the right thing for you. Incorporate this image for about a week into your prayer time. Seek to become conscious of the omni-present person of Jesus who said: **Lo, I am with you always, to the end of the age** (Matthew 28:20). Be open to experience the deeper reality within and beyond this representation. Keep a journal record of your encounter with Christ through the image. Remember, no person can ever be fully known by another. This is especially true of Jesus, the divine man. Be open to what you have known; and be willing to grow into awareness of God's self-representation through the Spirit.

2. **Another script for meditation** (An audio version is on the accompanying CD.) *This will be a time to look at your awareness of Jesus who is the divine man – our vital point of contact with God. Take a few moments to clear the mind of daily concerns by quietly letting thoughts go like clouds, until the mind clears into a luminous state of calm...Now invite pictures of the Lord to come into your awareness, as in an art museum. Walk around and look at several of them, and then find the one that seems most compelling and interesting. Just let your mind produce the right image...Now pull up a chair and sit before this image, and let it take shape and color and detail in your mind's eye...Can you identify this as a scriptural moment or is it out of context.? What is happening? Is Jesus alone? ...Since this is your picture, close your eyes and find yourself in the picture. Let this come alive by evoking each of your senses and by noticing a few details...Spend some time quietly in the Lord's presence without words.*

For Journaling (on option 1 or 2): *Write a journal entry about this experience (Or discuss it in your group). Describe in words as fully as you can, especially what Christ was like. This will continue to unfold as you write or share - really you are translating images to words. Notice your choice of scene and event. How did you see yourself in this picture?*

CHAPTER FIVE

THE ADULT
THE POWER TO HOLD & LEAD

TO DEATH AND BEYOND

Suddenly, one still autumn morning when I was almost eleven years old, my father died. My mother's voice calling to summon our neighbor, the doctor, shocked me awake. I ran downstairs, out the porch door, knelt on the flagstone floor and formed these words in my mind, *Dear God, if there is a God, don't let my daddy die* – but to no avail. This was the most intense moment of my childhood. Despair and alienation numbed my emotions. I not only felt, I also *became* bereft. Nothing would ever be the same.

Not long after, I had a dream, which then recurred from time to time. It was not a story, just a bare scenario: floating unhindered, and a dim awareness of being far out in space – boundless depth where I drifted past solid geometric figures. There were cubes, cones and pyramids - luminous, but mostly in shades of gray. During the months of being haunted by this dream, the empty, floating feeling gradually filled with fear. I sometimes awakened in a cold sweat. After many weeks I began hearing faintly from far off, a disembodied voice calling my name. I recognized my father's voice; it seemed odd to me that no meaning came across. I remember no reactive feeling or sense of connection, just a hollow sound, neither adding to my fear nor diminishing it. The dream did not come every night. But the final time, not far from my twelfth birthday, the dream came with fresh intensity. I was immersed in abysmal emptiness. I felt the familiar floating motion past luminous solid objects, going nowhere. Without meaning or sense of contact, the distant voice came closer. Loudly hearing my name, I woke with a start and only then knew the dream's message as clearly as if a light switch snapped on in my mind. I pulled the covers up to my neck and took to heart this revelation: *You are going to die at 8:45 on Friday evening three weeks from now.* There was no voice with this message, just the complete assurance it was true, and could in no way be avoided. At first I was terrified, the pinnacle of the fear that had been building with the many recurrences of the dream. I wanted to tell my mother, but did not; I thought it would upset her, and there was nothing she could do to change my fate.

Perhaps I got used to it, since the fear lessened after a few days. Two interesting things took place. One morning as I walked to school amidst falling leaves and a crisp autumn breeze, I noticed the familiar landscape of my mountain home. I mean, I really saw it as for the first time, evoking a meaning always there but unregarded. I sensed myself involved with the landscape and felt pure delight at what I saw. The other significant thing was also an unveiling of what was always there. Nothing happened or changed; but, one day at school, I looked differently upon the others, my peers and chums. I recall feeling peaceful and expansive. A certain distance arose like a buffer between other people and me. A layer of fear crumbled away like a sandcastle licked by the tide. I became aware of this fear only by contrast with the relaxed confidence that took its place. Again there emerged a new awareness: *My peers can no longer hurt me in any way, and what they think doesn't effect me a lot since I will soon be dead.*

This was the moment I became an adult, a young one, but nevertheless a grown-up with much more growth ahead. I remembered feeling forlorn after a playground scuffle in the second grade; the world, I thought, can't always be this dumb: there must be more to life than childhood offers. A hopeful idea came: *There will be more. Just wait.* At this moment four years later I knew the truth. Yes, this is more to my liking. Being grown up is like having new eyes.

By the time the appointed Friday rolled around I was happy as never before, involved with friends and interested in the usual round of things to do. Though circumstances had not changed at all, the world had become fresh and new. And though I was still sure death was coming for me, it didn't seem to matter. Starting to walk home from our school football game, I noticed the large clock on the scoreboard by the gates. The second hand swept past 8:45. Then there was a space of great clarity, like slipping around the edge of time. The same voiceless message that followed the dream continued to unfold: *This is it, you have died; that's all there is to it.* Since then I have never again feared death for others or myself. Though I have gone through much grief over the years, and have been close to many grieving persons, death itself has lost its sting for me. There came a certain freedom. Just as the bees that inevitably gather for a July picnic would still be annoying, but their presence would be easier to tolerate if there were no more reason to worry about their stingers.

Journaling Questions: *Was there a moment of awareness when you were no longer a child, or an adolescent (a significant graduation), or a spouse (after a divorce or being widowed)? Consider a period when it felt like you became something else, something different or something more. Possibly you experienced a traumatic event that seemed like turning a corner into another life. Locate your own critical moment. What was this like? What did you leave behind? What future did you anticipate? ...When you have located and described the event, dig a bit deeper by asking: What was the grief process like in making this transition? How was my relationship with God involved in this? Did my spiritual awareness and religious practice change? What have you learned about yourself in this transition? How and why have you grown?*

ENCOUNTER WITH JESUS AS LORD:
GOD'S POWER TO HOLD AND LEAD

On the next page is one of the oldest depictions of Christ. With minor variations it has been repeated in a multitude of versions, in widespread places, and over many centuries. It shows Jesus either enthroned or standing, half or full length. His left hand holds the scriptures, sometimes open with a key verse inscribed. His right hand is raised in blessing. (A liturgical blessing, by the way, is a gesture that symbolizes *touch*, with power to make contact, to influence the one blessed, and to communicate what it represents.)

The purpose of this image is to represent the Lordship of Jesus, who is *El Shaddai*, the Almighty. It is, like all images, a culturally produced

"Christ the Pantocrator" sketch for an icon

metaphor, in this case a symbol of ultimate spiritual power and effectiveness. "St. Patrick's Breastplate," an ancient Celtic hymn, expresses this talismanic spiritual strength in incantatory words, especially in the phrase: "**I bind unto myself today...the power of God to hold and lead**." Such is always the appropriate intention for one who prays before this aspect of Christ, which acknowledges that the Lord of the Church is at the heart of all things. The individual is invited to experience this truth directly by reverently accepting the holding and leading power of God from the unconscious center of our personal being. The enthroned Jesus is known by prayer, and from this place he guides the faithful in right paths. Book and blessing visually affirm **God's power to lead**. The throne, often portrayed, firm and immovable, visually shows **the power of God to hold** his creature in life. Direct experience of these twin powers is possible through deepening in spiritual life. This chapter seeks to open these two ways into the "throne room" of God.

++++++++++

Another classic *Pantocrator* icon, from Russia, the 16th Century Novgorod school, depicts Jesus seated before a rainbow of light (Rev.4:1-9) and holding the book open for all to read. This icon type is known as "The Enthroned Teacher." The text most frequently inscribed on this open book is **I am the light of the World;** but there are others. The wonderful Novgorod version is on the CD; on the next page is an old artist's pattern, a line drawing with blank space on the book, presumably for a choice of "words" to be inscribed.

Journaling Question: *What "word" do I see in the book? What is the Lord prescribing for me to savor, to "inwardly digest?" How do I feel about this?*

Very old sketch for a "Christ the Teacher" style Pantocrator

How to Find God's Power to Hold:
The Way of Sanctified Imagination

Meditation:
Tree of Life - A Journey into Depth

Blessed is the one who trusts in the Lord…this person is like a tree planted by a stream (Jeremiah 17:5-8).

Blessing comes from placing confidence in the source of life, in God. To be cursed is also to live, but in a parched and barren way, **like a shrub in the desert**, struggling to survive, but seldom fruitful. Let us use Jeremiah's imagery for meditation to place our trust where there is blessing.

Use CD or start music now -"*Water, Wind, & Stone*" is suggested. After "birdsong," begin script:

1. Breathing deeply, relax. Let us fully enter the realm of imagination. It is late summer and you are in a sunlit meadow beside a flowing stream.

2. Imagine a mature tree with spreading foliage, firmly rooted in the rich soil beside this stream. Now let your awareness move to the leaves and branches. Feel the sunlight warming the leaves...the breeze flows through the branches, touching every part, moving everything in various interesting patterns. Smell the breeze, sense the changing currents and temperature with your breathing...Notice the ripening fruit and think of what is coming to fruition in your life. Experience your gratitude for all this. ...

3. Let your awareness move toward the trunk; notice the bark, feel it, and then move within, ring by ring to the heart of this strong solid tree. This is the place of feeling, thought, reflection, choosing... Remembering a recent experience: what have you been about? What have you been pondering? What are your feelings about this? ...

4. Now put these matters aside, and let your awareness descend through the center into the root system. It is amazing, how much is hidden... the spreading roots, interacting with the soil in deep darkness. Enter the tap root and descend slowly to the deepest point where the root meets the underground waters ...and rest there without any other activity in this deep, dark place, as natural in its own way as the sunny world above. Just rest here for a few moments and get used to the darkness and quiet, as in an underground cave when the guide turns out the lights. You can hear only the muted movement of breathing. Experience the silence after the music of conscious experience is finished. Notice what this deep center is like. How would you describe its quality? ...You will be able to return here very often- at will, to an inner place more restful than sleep...Now return to the surface, and to your usual state of awareness.

Questions for Journaling & Sharing: What happened in this experience? What would I like to explore further? (This exercise with its three distinct levels is easier upon repetition.)

THE IMAGELESS WAY:
CONTEMPLATIVE PRAYER- A CENTRIPETAL FORCE

Silent prayer from the depths of human personality can only be described metaphorically. The sturdy tree, firmly grounded with roots taking in water, is a wonderful scriptural image for deep prayer at the point of contact of the human spirit with the Divine.

In our time there has been a proliferation of the practice known as *meditation*. There are similarities; but the different spiritual traditions of East and West vary considerably. In the Christian tradition, meditation usually refers to mental rumination with words and images (like the Jeremiah exercise above) that can sometimes lead into a deeper, wordless state, "resting in God." This deeper experience is known as *contemplation*. Perhaps the most familiar and helpful guide to this kind of prayer is the Centering Prayer Movement, popularized by Basil Pennington and his mentor Thomas Keating. There are numerous books, a website, and organized support groups for practitioners of this method. "Centering" is a metaphor suggested by the famous monk and writer Thomas Merton and the poet T.S. Eliot (Writing of Christ, Eliot said: "He is the still point of the turning world."). The current literature on contemplative practice is enormous; and it is assumed that users of this book will be, or will become familiar with helpful modern books, or even the medieval classics ("The Cloud of Unknowing," etc.), or eastern traditional practices such as Zen meditation or yoga. The contemplative path is surely the best road to an experienced-based grounding in God's "power to hold."

The following exposition of contemplative practice is based on the work of the late John Mains[4] who relies on Celtic spirituality's awareness of a personal God who "holds" the world in love, and on the unity of prayer and inspired action, symbolized by the simple "**Breathing Prayer**" outlined below. Mains advocates developing a still mind and deepening awareness in

---

[4]Books by John Mains for further exploration: **Words Into Silence,** N.Y., Paulist Press. 1981. **Letters From the Heart,** N.Y. Crossroads, 1982. **Moment of Christ,** N.Y.Crossroads, 1984. **The Present Christ,** N.Y. Crossroads, 1985. Audiotapes and further information about John Mains may be obtained from: 1) Christian Meditation Centre, 22 Campden Hill Rd. London W87DX, England (01-937-0014) and 2) The Benedictine Priory, West Montreal H361B3, Canada.

prayer by repeating a *mantra:* a prayer word or brief phrase. Anyone who has tried this method knows it is initially off-putting to most people, and can become an obsession for some. (*Mantras* should probably not be used by persons who have OCD.) But the *mantra* is generally useful and even necessary for most practitioners, just as wearing good sneakers is a good idea for runners. Chaos of the mind will be among the first experiences when sitting for silent prayer. One soon becomes aware of the noisiness and distraction when the mind is "taken out of gear" from the routine surface of work and pastimes. For this reason, teachers like John Mains have advocated plunging into the quiet pools of silence with the use of a *mantra* until we are, in the words of the poet Denise Levertov, "breathing the water." This will also be a tool for cleansing which Mains describes well:

> *"Persevering through this fidelity to the mantra, we then encounter a darker level of consciousness, of repressed fears and anxieties. The radical simplicity of the mantra clears this, too. But our first inclination is always to retreat from the dawn of self-knowledge... (Going beyond the entry into deep prayer, through the two levels of surface distraction and subconscious anxiety is like)... breaking through the sound barrier. When you come to that point there can be a lot of turbulence. It is at this moment that the discipline you have learned by saying the mantra and by faithfully continuing to say it, will enable you to be entirely open to the love of Jesus, which takes you through it."[5]*

The waking mind is gradually drawn down into a deeper awareness, a place of warm silence from which perseverance and passive cleansing will open out into direct experience of the eternal world. It is in this place that God comes to us in loving encounter. Sometimes one experiences the sense of Presence; sometimes it is the desire for that Presence. Either way, persevering in the discipline of daily quiet prayer with a prayer word can gradually transform a person by allowing the influence that comes only

---

[5] Neil McKenty, **In the Stillness Dancing,** Dorton, Lingman, & Todd. London, 1986.

from God to strengthen us from within.

A practical example of inner transformation is in the life story of the Right Reverend H.B. Dehqani-Tafti. As head of the Episcopal Church in Iran he was forced into exile in the Islamic revolution that overthrew the Shah some years ago. Bishop Dehqani-Tafti narrowly escaped assassination; his wife was severely wounded and their only son was killed. He writes from deep need and consequent blessing:

> *"Christians receive from God the power to carry out their mission in life. They get this power through prayer. I have always found prayer difficult, but I have never given it up completely. My main difficulty has always been lack of concentration. ...I greatly benefited about a year before the revolution from a course of twelve tape-recorded talks on meditation. ...They have been prepared by John Mains, a Benedictine father. ...The basis of the technique is to sit in silence twice a day, each time for not less than twenty minutes, repeating to oneself a short phrase from the Bible. Though I found this simplified the problem of concentration, it did not make it easier; indeed, real simplicity is always difficult to achieve. But at least I learned where I was; and I continued to persevere, sitting in solitude, and repeating what Fr. Mains calls a mantra, a word borrowed from Indian tradition. ...I now believe that God was teaching me this method of meditation to help me come face-to-face with myself. It worked like a vacuum cleaner, drawing out of my inner being everything that was consciously untrue. More and more, I came to realize...unless you are true to yourself, you cannot face difficulties and suffering creatively."*[6]

---

[6]H.B. Dehqani-Tafti, **The Hard Awakening,** pages 101-102, Triangle Books, London, 1981.

A Basic Contemplative Exercise:
Breathing Prayer

When you pray, enter your closet and when you have shut the door, pray to your Father who is in the secret place (Matthew 6: 6).

Do not use music for this kind of prayer. Just find a quiet, comfortable place free from distractions. Turn your phone off. Many people set a timer. To start, assume a comfortable, relaxed position. Then you may want to read or recall a verse or two of scripture in order to

Focus on God. The Psalms are especially good for this, or a single "word," or a passage such as ***The Lord is in His holy temple; Let all the earth keep silence before Him*** *(Habakkuk 2:20).*

Turn from your thoughts to awareness of your body. Your back should be straight, feet flat on the floor, a comfortable posture. (Other meditation postures are acceptable.) Consciously relax the stress in your body, especially any usual places of tension.

Breathe slowly and deeply from the diaphragm. Focus attention on the breathing: in-and-out; associate a *mantra* with breathing. Use something simple that you have chosen, such as the two syllables of the name of Jesus. (In slightly longer form, this is the "Jesus Prayer.") The mantra repetition need not be counted or used habitually. Return to it as needed to calm the mind and let go of any thought processes as you become aware of yourself thinking.

How to Find God's Power to Lead
Scripture Reflection: The Holy Spirit Leads

Sometimes people pray for the Holy Spirit without knowing what he wants to do with us. This is a real difficulty, because the relationship must always be cooperative and so it requires understanding. Much essential teaching about the Spirit is woven into other subjects in Jesus' long discourse at the Last Supper when he prepares his disciples for what is coming next. He tells them their relationship will continue, but it will change. The Holy Spirit will be the key to all this. The title used uniquely for God the Holy Spirit in St. John's gospel is *Paraclete*. This word is sometimes translated "advocate," someone called to be at one's side and on one's side in a court of law – a defense attorney. There is some legal flavor in Jesus' teaching in this passage, but it is not primary, and so the title is most often translated "helper" (not a strong enough word), or "comforter," (which at one time did not contain the sense of "comfortable"). We should probably get used to transliterating this title as we do a few other Biblical key words. It is very hard to translate without several qualifiers. A few key passages describe the Holy Spirit's operation:

If you love me, keep my commandments. And I will pray the Father, and he will give you another Paraclete, that he may abide with you forever - the Spirit of truth, whom the world cannot receive, because it neither sees him nor knows him; but you know him, for he dwells with you and will be in you. I will not leave you orphans; I will come to you (John 14:16-18)… **When the Paraclete comes, whom I shall send to you from the Father, the Spirit of truth who proceeds from the Father, he will bear witness of me** (John 15:26)… **It is to your advantage that I go away; for if I do not go away, the Paraclete will not come to you; but if I depart I will send him to you. And when he has come, he will convict the world of sin, and of righteousness, and of judgment** (John 16:7-8)…**When the Spirit of truth has come, he will guide you into all truth** (John 16:13)...**He will take what is mine and declare it to you. A little while, and you will not see me; and again a little while and you shall see me, because I go to the Father** (John 16:15-26).

In some ways, these passages speak clearly on their own about what the Spirit will do, and about his relationship with the Father, the Son and with those who believe. But in a few places, as with the word Paraclete, explanation will help. This passage speaks specifically about how God wants to guide us.

According to the larger context of St. John, Jesus is in complete harmony with the Father whom no one has seen. Jesus reveals God, makes God most clearly visible in redemptive love. (This is why the Passion narrative is paramount in each of the Gospels.) Jesus also wants to bring his disciples into a peer relationship with himself by disclosing God's intent. These friends would then be ready to carry on his work by the gift of the Spirit, who will be an ongoing aspect of Jesus' presence with his companions.

The Spirit, though one with Jesus, is distinct; and He will make Jesus real from within the disciples after his departure: **He will be in you.** The Holy Spirit who represents the Father and the Son will be discerned as the **truth** in all situations. He will lead those who are willing **into all truth**. He will do this by **convicting** us about the wrong course to pursue (**sin** means "missing the mark" or, in this context, disobeying Jesus' **commandment**). He also will **convince** us about the right path to take by giving us wise counsel (**judgment**). Through the mechanism of inspired conscience we may keep on course, and through the **abiding**, inward, spiritual presence of Jesus we may receive wisdom to know what we need to do in union with him and others.

What is spiritually essential, therefore, is: 1. to maintain a right relationship with God and others, 2. to keep the conscience strong and clear, and 3. to listen for the inner Christ the Lord who has God's power to lead. The first two essentials must always come before the third – intimacy, a clean heart, and then: "Follow the red thread."

A PERSONAL SHARING & JOURNALING:
INTIMACY AND RESISTANCE

Many years ago I was troubled over a series of choices to be made, and I found within a strong desire to do what was pleasing to God. In a period of prayer, struggling with this question, I was surprised by a sense of Presence. There was an interior light, warm and personal, not a vision exactly, except as of someone just around a corner. I intuitively recognized the presence of Jesus, though I had never before experienced anything like this. Thoughts came as flashes of insight, without words, on both sides of this straightforward conversation:

"Is that really you?" I said, and the issue became immediately unimportant.

The answer came: "Yes."

And I said, "Will you always be here?" - regretting already that such an experience of reality and joy might fade away.

But the answer was, "I have always been here. You just never wanted to be this close before."

I remembered that I had been baptized, connected to Christ, long ago as a child, and was dealing now not with the question of guidance but rather of who is the guide. My conclusion about this is that guidance generally comes to us more in a friendly rather than a parental intimacy with God.

My immediate response to this fuller relationship was a desire to do something to express my gratitude. "What can I do to show my love for you?"

There was a surprising, instantaneous answer: "Quit smoking."

To which my response was an immediate, "NO!"

This was indeed the Spirit of Truth revealing to me what would take many months to work out. When, eventually, my heart followed my mental commitment, I obeyed for the right reasons. Issues, including those about guidance, have over the years become less difficult.

Although the deepest desire of the human heart is unity with God, spirit to Spirit, one should be prepared to meet resistance. There is in everyone a stubborn place that does not want to take the right path. To recognize one's own resistance to following God is a significant accomplishment. God, in fact, convicts or convinces everyone who is open to this in such a way that we do not feel condemned, but instead we are amazed that what God requires of us, he also provides, given time.

For this reason sacramental confession is a powerful "means of grace," not to be neglected. The quest for guidance should often include a period of confessional prayer to establish a fresh contact with God, because without a right relationship, the sense of direction will be skewed. This may often be experienced as stressful double-mindedness; and so we must frequently cry out: **Create in me a clean heart, O God, and renew a right spirit within**

me (Psalm 51:10). The cleansing process may involve confessing specific wrongs that come to mind, or it may merely require quiet waiting until a sense of Presence or spiritual openness takes place. For guidance about matters that seriously affect one's direction in life, a retreat of several days would be helpful.

Since trust develops with practice, many will find the toughest issue involves intimacy, not how to find guidance or even to overcome resistance to it. When we are ready to deeply **Abide in Christ and He in us,** the issue of guidance may well become less problematic. The Holy Spirit may be known as the Guide more intimately than as a source of guidance. When the heart is reoriented, then the line of communication clears somewhat. It is only by maintaining a close relationship with God that we can expect to know what to do. The answer to the prayer "Show me the way, Lord," may be: "Come closer, and you will know." God's powers to hold and lead are intertwined.

In asking God for guidance, we realize we are fully known, in ways we do not know ourselves. Both our desire to follow the best path and our resistance to walking it are known to God, if not to the one praying.

Journaling Question: *Am I willing to know the truth that leads to freedom? In a specific area, or with regard to an unresolved issue, write about the will to move ahead and about whatever resistance may block the way. Offer what you have written as a prayer for help and guidance.*

A Personal Sharing & Journaling: "Finding the Red Thread"

Some time ago, in a period of personal transition, I sought out a respected spiritual director who I hoped would help me find the right path forward. (This, to me, was not the same as finding a suitable path, given the alternatives.) The general advice of H. Nouwen, to move positively in relation to self, others and God, was well known to me; but while useful, I felt the need of more specific direction. This warm and attentive, elderly counselor could or would not tell me what to do. I admit feeling disappointed that no clarity or advice came forth in a package to take home. (My heart actually became more restless after the meeting.)

Just as I prepared to leave he tossed off a reflection from his own spiritual journey that I have never forgotten: "Life has a Red Thread running through it which can always be found."

At first I considered this to mean that I should follow my intuition, play my hunches like a gambler. Though my mentor did not explain his meaning, my own interpretation has been: "Pray seriously, and then follow the most lively and life-giving hunch." This may well be a way to recognize and cooperate with the Holy Spirit. God's own shaping activity is, after all, woven somewhere into each of life's events. The "red thread" becomes a specific, recognizable sense of what to do next when one is living in intentional unity with God. Visions are not necessary and are rare, but one must be willing to trust God's guidance.

One thing we might add as essential to the character of God's guidance: to follow Christ in the power of the Spirit will involve moving more and more into the joy of finding one's true identity in serving the needs of others. Divine guidance is not another way of getting power for self-fulfillment in the sense "to get what I want." When we pray asking that we may grow up into the fullness of our aspirations, we are likely to find ourselves moving down into concern for the needs of others. Spiritual fulfillment is found only in self-abandonment.

Journaling Questions:

1. Intuition is the faculty that comes into play immediately when praying for guidance. What is my experience with finding and following my "hunches?" Am I willing, with God's help, to exercise and develop my sense of intuition?

2. The discernment of others is a necessary balance to the complete subjectivity of personal intuition. How does my sense of direction affect those who are close to me- my spouse, my family, and my pastor, for example? Am I willing to fully entrust my "guidance" to the discernment of those who are trustworthy and who share life with me?

A Personal Sharing and Guidance Model:
Moving with God's Wind

One of the strongest recommendations, when a person is seeking guidance, is to spend a few days listening for the Spirit's voice on a monastic retreat. Sometimes there are optional lectures provided by the nuns or monks. These may be called "conferences," or something else, and usually deal with personal prayer, the relationship with God, or personal concerns retreatants may bring up. On one such occasion I asked for advice about guidance, which I will pass along.

I mentioned there was a specific course of action I needed to decide about, and wanted help in finding the right path. The old monk said, without a moment's hesitation, "Always begin with prayer."

This was affirming, as I had prayed over this issue for several months. I knew myself willing by this time to take whatever path opened to me. My resistance had gradually cleared like fog as the morning sun hits it. Then the monk talked about the Holy Spirit working within our normal humanity: some persons, more visually oriented, get a picture of what should be done. Others are analytical and will make a plan, carefully considering pros and cons. Maybe some will have an urgent desire, a feeling or hunch that needs testing for substance and reality. The point is, God made us the way we are, and will guide each of us appropriately.

Then in his quiet but firm voice, the monk continued: "God will not expect you to do what is impossible; it may be difficult, but do-able with your abilities and resources; He always provides what He requires. It will be a partnership. But you must be willing to follow through as best you can."

This seemed to me practical and good advice. And as I thought and prayed about this, what I needed to do came to mind as a normal idea. Then a more urgent thought occurred to me; it seemed like the words of another: "You must plan to act." At once I felt confident; there was a sense of freedom, like a new door opening after undoing several locks and bolts. It seemed important to have gone through this process, and now not to look back; since I thought this might freeze me in mid course, like Lot's wife, who became a pillar of salt by the wayside.

To summarize, here is a concise procedure for seeking and finding guidance from God:

Beginning – **Prayer,**

> *Middle –* **Discernment,**

> > *And End –* **Action**

The details at each step will vary with the situation and issues – complex, simple, short or long. But it is a mistake to change the order of beginning, middle and end, or to omit one or two of these phases. There are those who never commit, or seem to act without careful consideration. There are those who plan and reconsider many times, while nothing changes. There are those who only pray in extreme peril, as a last resort; or they may pray only after the course has been planned. The path of wisdom is straightforward. When seeking spiritual guidance: **Ask, and it will be given to you; seek and you will find; knock and it will be opened to you** (Luke 11:9-13).

ADDITIONAL INSIGHTS FROM JOHN MAINS ON PRAYER[7]

"Our prayer is not to concoct some prayer of our own. Our prayer is to become present through silence and in faith to the prayer of Jesus rising from the core of the heart to the Father." Page 84.

Imagination can be an enemy in prayer: "the more we think about, picture or stir up imagination for autonomous visions of him. This is not to denigrate theology, philosophy or art. But these fruits of our minds and hearts have value for ultimate meaning only so far as they *clarify, encourage,* or *purify* (Italics mine, because imagination is essential at these points.) our journey to the frontiers of the limited human consciousness. On

---

[7] All quotations are from Neil McKenty, **In the Stillness Dancing, the Journey of John Mains**, Darton, Longman & Todd, London, 1986.Used by permission.

this frontier we are met by a Guide who is unlimited by human consciousness, the Person of Jesus Christ...All Christian prayer is a growing awareness of God in Jesus...And for this growing awareness we need to come to a state of undistraction, to a state of attention and concentration – that is, a state of awareness...The only way I have been able to find to come to that quiet, to that undistractedness, to that concentration, is the way of the mantra..." Pages 84-85.

The mantra Fr. Mains strongly suggests to be used is "**Maranatha, Come, Lord Jesus.** (Revelation 22:20). Say it...in your mind...listen to the sound of it."

But he also writes of other choices: "Each repetition (of "Abba" – as little children to their father) is a new confidence established – not because the child *thinks* about it, but because the child experiences the relationship as *real*. That is what mantra is about - no thought, no imagination; only *presence*." Page 86.

John Mains died on December 30, 1982. Aware of his own hastening physical death, he wrote in a newsletter article dated 12/8/82, of the end in the beginning, realized eventually in death: "The mystery surrounding Jesus was perceptible from the beginning of his life. Not until his death and resurrection was it capable of being fully apprehended, fully known. Because not until then was it completed. Our life does not achieve full unity until it transcends itself and all limitation by passing through death." Page 188.

Discovering the Treasure Within

CHAPTER SIX

THE ADULT
WHOLENESS & BELIEVING

TINA SPROCKETT GETS THE WHOLE STORY

This is Tina Sprockett reporting from just outside the Globe Theater where the latest play from the pen of Master Will Shakespeare has just now had its premier performance. It is a tragedy about a pair of infatuated teens from warring Italian families. Romeo and Juliet find they cannot endure the harsh realities of their world. They are, as it were, "star-crossed." Does this play have a future? Or will Will withdraw it in favor of his blockbuster, "Titus Andronicus?" – It's always a draw for the crowd that flocks here near the bridge for the great action and adventure of bear-baiting. But let's hear from some randomly selected members of the audience: "Well ma'am, what did you think of the show?"

"It was just sensational. The Juliet was so delicate and cute in the blue gown she wore in the balcony scene. You just knew Romeo was inspired to say those lovely things about Juliet and the sun by the glint of her silken blond hair. And when they kissed for the first time, I positively got goose bumps. And finally at the end when he kissed her and died, it was so intense I still have a knot in my stomach. This is a show that just grabs you and won't let go."

"And what was your reaction?"

"Well I'm still thinking there must have been a way to send those two off to Capri just after the wedding, but then one can't have a tragedy with a happy ending, can one? I wonder if there really is a concoction that can put you in suspended animation like that. That would be lovely indeed –well, not really –very hard to figure out when you would wake up and such. I knew things weren't going to work out during the sword fighting early on. These two families were badly out of control, what could you expect from their wild children? Typically passionate Italians! I knew they weren't going to think of a way to resolve the conflict. Those teens were just pawns, too young and helpless to find a strategy to get what they want and move on."

"And you two?"

"Well we don't think this is a good story for children –too much violence and gore. And certainly we shouldn't be showing that suicide is ever an option when you can't get what you want."

"Now dear, it's really parents who should learn from –Capulets and Montagues, hah! Some one ought to give them parenting lessons. It just shows more attention should be paid to supervising the children. If they hadn't left everything up to the Nurse and that meddling Fr. Whatsits things would have turned out differently. Actually every parent should see this show, either as a warning or as reassurance they're doing a decent job."

"And you Miss; what did you think of R & J?"

"I don't really know. It was sooo saad! I just had this feeling of impending doom from the beginning. And then everyone was very angry. And then such delicate and tender passion –first love, it was like those lovely words had music even when no one was singing. This play was really an emotional fencing match, where the "unkindest cut of all" comes at the end. Quite touching really."

"Sir, you stand out a bit in your Chinese costume. Are you an actor, or a tea merchant come to see a bit of Shakespeare?"

"Good guess, miss. I sell silks. I had some tickets in exchange for material for the ladies' wardrobe. You know, I never think British humor is funny. Why Shakespeare's Falstaff character is so popular in London mystifies me. This show was better, though Chinese children would never think they could do what they want and disrespect their parents like that. Incredible plot. Never play in China. The main characters I thought unbelievably silly, but I loved the costumes; and I still try to figure you English out."

"I think we have time for one more viewpoint. You please."

"Well I found this whole thing amazing, that Shakespeare could have all these characters in his head. It's such a big world populated by one man's imagination. His women seem real; his characterizations, like whole persons. I get the impression one could see the play over and over and still find new things within it. Hopefully this playwright will try his hand at other couple tragedies as well, about adults next time."

"Sorry our time is up folks. It seems everybody has a different point of view, and there are so many people milling around as the crowd breaks up; we can't interview them all. But it does appear this show will be in for a long run here at the Globe.

This is Tina Sprockett signing off for now."

+++++++++++

In this story the speakers are so distinct, it would be hard to imagine them communicating with each other or agreeing about anything, even about what they had in common, such as the first experience of the same play. Then if, as for the Chinese man, another culture comes into play, there is a further barrier to understanding. But people have always known that different as we are, these differences are limited. Several systems of personality types have been proposed, along with theories of how we all got to be the way we are. For most of pre-scientific Western history, the four "humors" thought to flow through the body theoretically accounted for major types of people; there were choleric, phlegmatic, melancholic and sanguine persons. Though these have absolutely no biological basis, and made for bizarre medical treatments, there are still distinctly spiritual lessons to be learned from this theory.[8]

In the mid 20th Century, Carl Jung's theory of personality types became widely used. He thought there were four basic orientations toward life; these were grounded, probably not in biology, but in behavioral tendencies and early childhood choices. The "Tina Sprockett" story above contains each of the Jungian personality types sketched according to the unique ways they might express themselves. The chart on the following page summarizes the distinctions:

---

[8] Note e.g. Ole Hallesby, Temperament and the Christian Faith, Augsburg, 1978

PREFERENCES ARE FOR:	ORIENTATION TO LIFE, CONCERN;	REVEALED IN SELF-EXPRESSION BY:
Sensation	That something is	Clear description of facts
Thinking	What something is	Analytic concern for meaning
Feeling	Is it agreeable or not	Judgments based on values
Intuition	Whence it came, where going	Concern for the big picture

Jung's understanding of personality types is just a bit more complicated, because these distinctions are made according to this chart of preferred ways of doing things:

E: If I am *Extroverted*, then into the outer environment of people, things, various activities

or

I: If *Introverted*, then into the inner world of concepts and ideas

S: If by *Sensation*, gathering facts, trusting details, preferring present reality

or

N: If by *Intuition*, finding patterns, possibilities and meaning, more future oriented

T: If by *Thinking*, then my approach is objective, considering pros and cons, and the logical outcomes

or

F: If by *Feeling* approach, subjectively, from within the situation applying personal values, seeking harmonious outcomes

J: The *Judging* person prefers to have structure, run the world, to get decisions made

or

P: The Perceiving person prefers to remain open to situations as they arise, to be open-ended and adaptable

Into which world does my energy flow?

How do I perceive reality (gather data/info)? Through the *Perceiving Functions*:

How do I make decisions? By using the *Judging Functions:*

Jung thought these distinctions were universal and fairly easy to make. A popular short questionnaire (The Meyers-Briggs Personality Type Inventory or MBPTI) has been widely used in business, education, and counseling so that very many people can describe themselves with four letters (The author for example is an ENFP type.) But what should we do with those borderline people who are not so typical?

And then further research and analysis has resulted in more complex theory, as anyone having attended an "Enneagram" workshop will know. There are other theories of personality type, but to this point, though the tools are useful for understanding self and others, research has been uncertain. Carl Jung himself thought the basics of personality type were available to common-sense thinking because they were manifestations of the conscious parts of the *Self.* It is likely that even without taking a personality preference test; one could review the distinctions above, and give oneself a four letter description after acknowledging habitual preferences. Try picking one from each pair of distinctions, from left to right:

Extroverted Intuitive Thinking Perceiving

E N T P

- OR-

I S F J

Introverted Sensing Feeling Judging

There are six personality types written into the Tina Sprockett story. Perhaps one of them reminds you of yourself! As you look over your journaling, which of these voices are prominently present?

For Journaling: As an ENFP, I have noticed that many in my profession share my personality type; that my spouse is easier to understand since we know our types and take our differences into account; and that my nemesis (and challenge to grow) is usually one of those people who are my opposite type, those "pesky" ISTJs. For a journaling exercise you may want to *describe your version of each of the four letters you have come up with.* Like primary colors, our tendencies when mixed and varied, take on rich hues. If, like me, you are an ENFP, we may be similar in some ways, but what is most important is that we are unique. No one ever does the human dance the same way. And we become more distinctly ourselves as we mature.

In a second entry, *think of some people who are your opposite type: Have you found them curious, interesting, weird, or threatening? How have you managed to communicate, or failed to communicate with these persons?*

MORE JOURNALING EXERCISES: AIMING FOR WHOLENESS

Growth toward wholeness, involves several distinct tendencies of the soul. Each of these should be noted in a journal reflection. (*In this situation, I tend to...*)Then see if one of these is especially compelling for you at this time. *Reflect further on how you might move with prayer and action into that spiritual work:*

Wholeness begins with adult self-acceptance. We need to happily know who we are and work at being the best possible version of that person. There is the old story about the Rabbi Mendel who often compared himself in prayer to various saintly others, no doubt with much penitent humility. To him the Lord replied, "It will be enough to be the best possible Rabbi Mendel."

Journaling Question: *What have I done, what can I still do to fully develop and utilize my personal strengths?*

Only Jesus is the perfectly balanced whole human being. But by growing in his likeness, we will move toward completion. The first part of life is the natural time to develop our strengths and enthusiasms, our natural gifts. But humans should never stop growing. Eventually comes the time to develop our "minor suits," the things others do well, maybe even easily, but we have not been able to do or can't imagine doing. One thinks of the disorganized, spontaneous person who has succeeded by moving from one thing to another while others pick up the clutter. Or consider the accountant who always wanted to be in a rock band. Or there is that caregiver who never lets anyone do much for them. We all would have examples. The instances that occur to you will not be accidental. Use your own examples to look at what they indicate about growth opportunities you may be missing.

Journaling Question: *What are my minor suits? Should I learn to play them?*

One of the best ways to learn about and transform weak or undeveloped qualities is to note these things in people we admire. Instead of saying, "She does that, but I never could." say to yourself, "I can't be her, or do what she has done well for so long; but I can find something like that in myself, forget my excuses, and begin to develop it." Maybe such a person would give you some pointers or act as a mentor.

For Journaling: *Write and pray about this possibility.*

The most widely accepted *ego* trait put forward by Carl Jung involved the distinction between the Introvert and the Extrovert. Everyone is a bit of both in self-estimation; but Jung's definition is helpful, not to be used as a self-labeling stereotype, but for self-awareness leading to growth. The extrovert is energized by the company of others. That person comes back from a social event ready for more. The introvert, by comparison in this situation feels drained, needing to recover. Think of yourself in social situations. Are you usually drained or energized by them? Whichever the case may be, this is part of who you are. It is a good idea to accept this basic personality assessment and act accordingly. But growth is always an option for the maturing adult. This involves moving toward balance. A shy person may take careful steps to move into more intense social settings, one step at a time; and will also plan a suitable recovery period. The life of the party may be challenged to take some time to be alone, just to become better at the skills and joys of solitude; but don't sabotage this by making small talk with all the people at the retreat center. An excellent personal Bible study about this personality issue would be to consider the stories about Jesus' three friends from Bethany. We know little about Lazarus, but his sisters Mary and Martha are among the purest examples of introversion and extroversion. After Lazarus' death, for example, Martha hastened to confront Jesus about her concerns; Mary, on the other hand, stayed behind. Read about these opposite persons, who surely must have struggled to charitably live together. (Luke 10:38-42 and then read John 11:1-41, a very different story; but the same personalities are etched for us in just a few words.)

Journaling Questions: In what ways are Martha and Mary different? Which one reminds me most of myself? Thinking of my siblings, who of us was more or less introverted/extroverted? What difference did that make in what they did and how they did it? *Does this pattern still affect my life? Is this behavior appropriate in my current social situations?*

Also for Journaling: *Where would I place myself on a scale of 1-10 moving between introversion and extroversion? Has my sense of this changed over the years? In which direction should I move at this time? How can I begin to make that move? Are there others who would support me in trying some new behavior? Are there some who would try to prevent these changes?*

One of Jung's premises is that the soul of a person is embodied in an image of the opposite sex. This *animus* or *anima* is also the opposite personality type from that of the conscious self, the *ego*. The implication of this, for how a person should structure the life of prayer, is significant. Extroverts will need silent times of solitary retreat, for example. Introverts should consider small group Bible sharing and supportive group retreats.[9]

---

[9] Useful detailed advice about different styles of prayer for different personality types is available in Prayer and Temperament, Chester R Michael & Marie C. Norrisey, The Open Door, Inc., Charlottesville, 1984

SCRIPTURE REFLECTION:
THE WHOLE WORLD AT THE FOOT OF THE CROSS

Salvation is for all kinds of people, not just for the spiritual or for the gravely wicked. It is a process by which God participates fully in our need and brings us into a new life which we are incapable of finding by our own efforts. Salvation is about life after life, but that begins from whatever is our point of need. Eternity always begins now. Jesus explains in the Gospel According to John: **When I am lifted up from the earth, I will draw everyone to my self. This he said to signify by what death he would die** (John 12:32-33). This passage refers to Jesus' giving himself up in perfect love (Remember John 15:13.); but the word translated "lifted up" is also the word for "raised up." In John's gospel, the dying and rising of Jesus are understood as two parts of the same redemptive action. This action is an accomplished fact: **By his wounds we *have been* healed** (I Peter 2:24). *Healed* can also be translated, *made whole* or *saved*. The consequences of salvation are yet to come in fullness, still they are always contemporary – specific signs of the new life available now.

In this section we will consider the encounter with Jesus as **Savior**, the one "lifted up" to "draw everyone" to God. We will reflect on the story of Jesus' death not by reading through John's passion narrative, but by prayerfully examining the traditional portrayal of the scene in the Russian icon sketch above. (The marvelous 1360 Novgorod version is on the accompanying CD).

There are different emphases expressed by means of the several classic images. The tortured and bloody Christ from Colmar by Grunewald, for example, shows solidarity with our illnesses and physical pain. Various images are for meditation at specific Stations of the Cross. Some Orthodox icons portray more historical detail, such as the two thieves, several women, multiple soldiers, or grieving angels. This image from Novgorod does not tell the story; it suggests: it gently and quietly presents the fact of salvation and its consequences, its fullest meaning: **It is finished** (John 19:30). This is from the perspective of the fourth gospel, as understood within the Eastern Church, but is universally recognized among Christians.

The scene is Calvary, the place of the skull, a place of crucifixion outside the walls of Jerusalem. At the foot of the cross is a skull which locates the event; but it surely represents the death of everyone; traditionally this is said to be the skull of Adam, the typologically *primal* and *representative* human person; Adam will also be symbolically important in the Easter icon. This symbol represents humanity identified redemptively with the dying and rising Christ. The event is eternal, Good (or *God's*) Friday, not just the historic day of Jesus' execution. This icon of Christ emphasizes not the horrendous political and human aspect of this event, but God's involvement in it; and so attention focuses on the majesty and serenity of Jesus who has accomplished his mission: **It is finished.** And so, prayerful reflection on this image does not deny or inflame our emotional reaction like much "realistic" art does; it quiets and deepens the response. As such this image is especially suitable for meditative journaling.

There are many wonderful records of such journaling and its effect, such as Dame Julian of Norwich's *Showings*. But let us take a near contemporary example. Fr. Andrew, an English monk and parish priest, was one of the great holy men of the World War II generation. He offered spiritual comfort to the British people assaulted by the uncertainty and upheavals of war. Here is a personal letter he wrote April 7, 1945, Good Friday:[10] It is the fruit of a deep experience of imaginative, meditative prayer. Fr. Andrew gives voice to the crucified Christ who has power to draw all people to himself:

I made a record of my experience. I have copied it for you: As I beheld Him in his silent majesty, hanging upon his cross, with the eyes of my soul I saw in his gaze upon this world from his place of pain, that there was no smallest trace of reproach, complaint, or blame, but only unutterable, overwhelming love.

I saw that his love was our judgment; that as the eye must quail before the light of the sun because of the exceeding brightness of the light, so the soul must quail before him because of the exceeding splendor of his love; and that love was the greatest of all forces, the perfection of all power.

Then there came to me three distinct messages.

---

[10]Father Andrew, *Letters*, page 118

The first to <u>all the world</u>: His love went forth from him in silent power but his silence said, with greater clearness than any spoken words, "Your sin has never lessened my love; here on the cross I love you with an everlasting love."

The second was to <u>all sufferers</u>: "I am God. Suffering is not natural to me; as God I cannot suffer, but when I gave to certain of my creatures free wills and they admitted selfishness and sin into my universe, then of necessity there followed suffering, and suffering can only leave my universe when sin has departed from it. But when I saw my creatures suffering, I took upon me a human nature that I might make their suffering my suffering. All the suffering of the world is my suffering; I have made it mine in love; they that love me may make my suffering theirs."

The third was to <u>all the disillusioned, disappointed, bereaved and out of heart:</u> "Behold me. Here I am dying in the dark, and I come to bring light to the world. I am dying at the hands of hate, and I come to bring love to the world. Death is closing in upon me, and I come to bring life to the world. But I remain true to my faith; dying in the dark, I believe in the Light; killed by hate, I trust Love; with death closing in upon me, I believe in life; on the third day I shall rise again. Do you then cling to your ideals; in any darkness, still trust the Light; in any hatred, still trust Love, and be sure that, though all consciousness be slipping from you and you yourself seem to be sinking into a void, eternal life is yours."

'So the message was given, and the silence was full of peace. God bless and keep you.'

Andrew

The death of Christ has definite messages that are universal; and yet as above and in your journaling, there can be special *words* for this moment, situation and even personality. Jesus' redemption is always to be experienced at the specific point of need; that vulnerable place is each person's interior point of encounter with the saving power of Christ. He meets us where we really need him; He is always there before we are willing to recognize the need for a savior. And this redemptive love meets different types of people in their own ways. Only God could accomplish this!

The Crucifixion icon we are considering includes two men and two women. Other versions of the image are more literally portrayed *visual readings* of the text of John which mentions three women - also Mary, "his mother's sister, the wife of Clopas" (John 19:25). Since the subject is universal salvation, and in the light of the four-fold personality theory of former times, it seems apparent these four are singled out for meditative attention to suggest pictorially how Jesus, through the cross, is working out of the plan of salvation for different sorts of people. He is the One, beyond time and at each saving moment, who draws **everyone** to Himself as universal savior. The pre-scientific theory of different types of personalities, as mentioned before, included the sanguine, the melancholic, the choleric and the phlegmatic personalities. It seems likely that the icon represents human variety in this way, balancing men and women and including a significant *gentile*, a person from beyond the pale of Jewish culture. Whether there are four *types* of people, according to whatever theory we use to consider this, may not be as important spiritually so much as the message: His outpoured love draws everyone, but differently. If there were a thousand types of persons, Jesus' sacrifice would be sufficient, with none excluded!

In journaling about coming to Christ as savior, put yourself in the place of one of these persons who reminds you of your way of being human. (Or perhaps you will be a fifth person standing prayerfully before "the exceeding splendor of the love…the perfection of all power.")

1. One of the holy women, almost certainly to be identified as Mary Magdalene, is portrayed as deeply emotional. Usually, as in this version, she is clothed in red; possibly to indicate a sanguine personality, capable of excesses of temper, but also of heartfelt devotion. At the resurrection she is first to see the risen Lord. No doubt her tears are spiritually important. Isaac the Syrian (4th Century), and others after him especially in the East have

considered the "gift of tears" to be a result of "the baptism of the Holy Spirit' – the means by which the believer is cleansed inwardly and united with Christ. In our culture where tears are often considered a sign of weakness, this spiritual gift may be blocked to our detriment. For some, acceptance of the emotional element in religion and various expressions of that behavior may be an important part of their spiritual journey. *Whether or not you identify with this woman, consider the emotional aspect of your spiritual experience, or the lack of that dimension. Is expressive emotion an important part of who you are, or a product of cultural conditioning?* This would be a good question for self-examination by journaling and discussion.

2. The "beloved disciple," usually identified as John (Who knows which John!), is portrayed as an inward, thoughtful person, a melancholic, like Hamlet. He is the only one of Jesus' twelve disciples who stood close to the cross, the one to whom Jesus entrusted the care of his mother. John is gentle and reflective. Christ honors those qualities. It seems likely that this man's capacity for intimacy has something to do with the unique flavor of the gospel tradition he transmitted to the later church. He is the "beloved disciple," the model of discipleship who leaned closest to Jesus at the Last Supper, the only one of the Twelve at the foot of the cross. This is the strand of apostolic tradition that teaches us about communion with God, and invites us to experience it in a new way. Jesus plans to share *his* close relationship with God: **Yet a little while and the world will see me no more, but you will see me. Because I live, you will live also. On that day you will know that I am in my Father, and you in me, and I in you** (John 14:19-20). *Do you have to fight depression, and yet yearn for a deeper relationship with God? Do you feel at home in the Gospel of John?*

3. The other man in this icon is the soldier tradition has called Longinus (a gentile, of course). With the others he carried out Christ's execution. Yet he was also the first to proclaim: **Truly this man was the Son of God** (Mark 15:39). He has the qualities an earlier pre-psychological Christian culture used to describe the choleric person. Like all of us, he needs a savior to be his better, godly self. He is a practical, dutiful man, capable of cruelty

perhaps; but also a person of action, open to testing and accepting new truth. *Are you, in some ways, this person with similar strengths, weaknesses and potential for growth?*

4. Finally there is Mary, our Lord's mother. Perhaps we can say she is phlegmatic: a calm, consistent person deeply affected by the actions of others. She points, as always, even in her overwhelming grief, beyond herself to the Truth she carried in her womb. *Do you have Mary's way of relating to the world? Can you identify with her joys and sorrows?*

These traditional personality types, and also the typology of Carl Jung or of other more current psychological, business and spiritual teachers, are likely never to be accepted without reservations as fully accurate models for thinking about ourselves and others. The point is that the whole persons for whom Christ died are distinctly different. And since He died for everyone, he can carry God's love to each person, in just the right manner.

JOURNALING EXERCISE: AT THE CROSS

*If there is one of these persons at the foot of the cross with whom you strongly identify, project yourself into that personality, or perhaps be a fifth person, placing yourself in the picture, before the mystery of redemption. Write a reflection that expresses your sense of need for salvation (Do you relate to this in terms of **wholeness, forgiveness, healing, acceptance, strength**, etc.?) Be as specifically self-descriptive as you can. Ask God to accept you just as you are. Let yourself be touched by the perfect love the Father has to give you through his Son. Hear the words for yourself, "I am lifted up to draw you to myself." Does some response to God's love arise within you? Write a letter to God, expressing your thoughts and feelings.*

GUIDED MEDITATION:
THE TRANSFORMATION- COMING TO LIFE IN CHRIST

Jesus explained his upcoming dying and rising with a simple metaphor from nature. **Unless a grain of wheat falls into the ground and dies, it**

remains alone; but if it falls into the ground and dies, it brings forth much fruit (John 12:24). Dying to increase in life is not an entirely unnatural idea: thus, the nature symbols associated with Easter and springtime. The following meditation involves an imagined cocoon. Unlike other meditations in this book, participants, even if doing it alone, should be prepared to move around, not just in the mind's eye. Later journaling and/or discussion will include reflection on this non-verbal experience.

(This script should be used with recorded music: strongly suggested - "Appalachian Spring" by Aaron Copland. An audio version with music is on the CD.)

Lie comfortably on the floor with space enough to move around without bumping into obstacles...1. After a period of quiet relaxation, use imagination and fantasy to enter into a unique, personal **cocoon.** *Inside you will feel secure, warm and content...Experience your cocoon fully. See it from inside, touch and smell, and listen to the pulse of life from within. Enjoy this moment...2. Now the cocoon becomes cramped; it's time to break out. Keep your eyes closed and act this out by carefully and slowly moving to stand up...3. Then with eyes still shut, find your balance, and explore the freedom of this new position just a bit...Now you have been transformed. You are a new creature. Let this new being take shape fully. Again use all your senses. What is it like? ...Take some time to fully experience...* (As the music nears its quiet end)... *Now you will come gently and gradually back to this time and place .Be seated if you wish....and open your eyes.*

For Reflection: Make a brief journal entry, and then share in group without comment on the first, then second question: 1. What happened in each of the three phases of this exercise? 2. Is there anything about my life that is cramped and uncomfortable, something I need to let go in order to find, and to manifest whatever I am becoming from within? When all have finished, discuss what you have shared. For a person journaling without group sharing, a good outline would be: *Reflecting on the nonverbal experience, describe the old self...then the new self...And then, consider how to get from here to there.*

SCRIPTURE REFLECTION:
FOUR FAITH ENCOUNTERS WITH THE RISEN SAVIOR

In this image the risen Jesus is drawing Adam and Eve first, and then a train of others to himself. He shares the power of his Resurrection. The primal couple represents our full humanity. Christ destroys the gates of death. Notice the variety of keys. Jesus has taken captivity captive, and unlocked all the doors that restrain us spiritually, by demolishing the gates of sin and death. This is a classic representation of the traditional Easter message. When Jesus touches us in the midst of our need, he never leaves us the same. He raises us up into a new way of living and acting. He empowers us with his Spirit. With the act of faith (called "belief" in the Gospel of John) the Christian's new life begins, and then it continually develops.

Like a muscle, faith requires exercise. Then it grows and matures, characterizing the spiritual adult. (*Faith* is Paul's term, *believing* is John's; overlapping in meaning, but each with its own nuances.) **These things are written that you may believe that Jesus is the Christ, the Son of God, and that believing you may have life in his name** (John 20:31). Faith, or believing, is more than intellectual assent; it is the inner capacity that Jesus awakens in us so that we can become fully alive with Him. Here are four stages in the process of faith development as presented in the fourth gospel's stories of encounters with the risen Jesus:

1. *The process of awakening faith.* **Now on the first day of the week Mary Magdalene went to the tomb early, while it was still dark, and saw that the stone had been taken away from the tomb. Then she ran and came to Simon Peter, and to the other disciple, whom Jesus loved, and said to them, "They have taken away the Lord out of the tomb, and we do not know where they have laid Him." Peter therefore went out, and the other disciple, and were going to the tomb. So they both ran together, and the other disciple outran Peter and came to the tomb first. And he, stooping down and looking in, saw the linen cloths lying there; yet he did not go in. Then Simon Peter came, following him, and went into the tomb; and he saw the linen cloths lying there, and the handkerchief that had been around His head, not lying with the linen cloths, but folded together in a place by itself. Then the other disciple, who came to the tomb first, went in also; and he saw and believed** (John 20: 1-8).

The first experience of God beyond death is spiritual emptiness, a silence that is alive. This is the potential, the openness, within any situation. In this encounter Mary Magdalene, Simon Peter and "the other disciple" found in the experienced absence of Jesus - signs of God. Notice that this happened in different ways to each of the three. Only the **other disciple** perceived the emptiness and then responded with faith. The act of God breaking into our darkness is obscure at first, like the very soft beginning of some music. In the tuned acoustic of a concert hall we could hear it. But with the less sensitive amplification of an electronic system, we strain to hear, as we may miss the first bars of such quiet music. A few people, like this disciple, are especially sensitive to spiritual things. Most of us are only able to develop this sensitivity by the regular practice of silence and solitude. These are ways to withdraw from the babbling flow of life and especially from habitual expectations.

In this story Mary expected to anoint the body and continue to grieve: quite to be expected. What did Peter anticipate? Perhaps he sought concrete evidence for himself in order to know what action to take. Both of these persons reacted initially to the empty tomb with disappointment and frustration, but differently. Only the unnamed disciple heard the first phrases of the new music; he believed, though he came to the facts second. This is that faith that is prior to understanding. The faith God draws out of the "cave of the heart" is present in the subconscious before it comes into awareness. Waiting in darkness can sometimes be most helpful in preparing to find the response of faith. It is a legitimate state of soul that calls to mind what St. John of the Cross described as "the dark night." God touches us and leaves us with a sense of longing, unfocused desire without fulfillment or consolation. This burst of spiritual light is blinding and requires a period of time for the soul to adjust to the uncreated light of Christ. At first the darkness deepens; a purifying process of refocusing takes place. The poet Gerard Manley Hopkins came to faith and then passed many years with little spiritual consolation. Yet his spiritual sensitivity grew and he continued to act faithfully to fulfill his active calling. "There lives the dearest freshness deep down things" was his finely crafted insight taken from years of groping along in dark faith.

For journaling: *Remember a desolate period in your life –perhaps a time of grief, brokenness or disappointment. Revisit this time and see if you can detect the earliest moments of rising new life. As Hopkins did, you may notice something "deep down things," if you dig courageously into your memories.*

2. *Faith continues to develop.* Mary stood outside by the tomb weeping, and as she wept she stooped down and looked into the tomb. And she saw two angels in white sitting, one at the head and the other at the feet, where the body of Jesus had lain. Then they said to her, "Woman, why are you weeping?" She said to them, "Because they have taken away my Lord, and I do not know where they have laid Him." Now when she had said this, she turned around and saw Jesus standing there, and did not know that it was Jesus. Jesus said to her, "Woman, why are you weeping? Whom are you seeking?" She, supposing Him to be the gardener, said to him, "Sir, if you have carried him away, tell me where you have laid him, and I will take him away." Jesus said to her, "Mary!" She turned and said to him, "Rabboni!" (Which is to say, Teacher). Jesus said to her, "Do not cling to me, for I have not yet ascended to my Father; but go to my brethren and say to them, "I am ascending to my Father and your Father, and to my God and your God." Mary Magdalene came and told the disciples that she had seen the Lord, and that he had spoken these things to her (John 20: 11-18).

Now the risen Christ is fully present, but unrecognized. Without further input from outside, Mary Magdalene is stuck, like the Pharisees at the Gospel's outset who were close to Jesus, but did not know it. (John the Baptist pointed him out: **There is one among you whom you do not recognize** [John 1:26]). The Magdalene cannot by her own effort move from a disappointing conversation with the supposed gardener to a fulfilled partnership with God through Christ. (Remember Jesus had said: **No one has seen God at any time.** But he also said: **One who has seen me has seen the Father** [Jn.14:9]) Mary's faith is quickened beyond the experience of absence, when Jesus calls her by name. She immediately responds with recognition and is able to accept the call to leave the moment of awakening and to do an errand for the Lord. She joyfully acts in obedience. Obedient action also comes before the fuller faith which includes understanding. "Some things must be believed before they can be seen," as the slogan has it. In the faith journey, the Lord tends to reveal just enough to let us recognize who he is and that he is with us; then we receive a message: something to do on his behalf. Though faith is an inward awareness, it can not be separated from action. **Faith without works is dead**, says James 2:17. For faith to continue to develop, we should be prepared to act obediently.

The boy Samuel is an excellent example of persistence in this stage of faith. He had never heard God's voice directly; and so when the Lord called the boy's name in the night, Samuel did not know what he was hearing. It took three trips to his mentor, old Eli, for the boy to recognize the voice of God calling from the depths of night. Then he said, as Eli suggested, "Speak Lord, for your servant is listening." God spoke and Samuel did as he was instructed. (See 1 Samuel 3 for the whole story.)

For Journaling: *Sift back through your memories. Notice if there have been occasions when you were addressed by God; whether or not you did anything about it at the time, or were even aware of this sort of possibility. Consider each instance and ask if and how the Holy Spirit drew from you an obedient response. Now move to the present and see if God has been speaking to you in some way and what action you are supposed to take. (Understanding will usually come later, if at all. Still this reflection may open you to insights and fuller awareness.)*

3. _Steps toward a "closer walk with God"_. The same day at evening, being the first day of the week, when the doors were shut where the disciples were assembled, for fear of the Jews, Jesus came and stood in their midst, and said to them, "Peace be with you." When he had said this, he showed them his hands and his side. Then the disciples were glad when they saw the Lord. So Jesus said to them again, "Peace be to you! As the Father has sent me, I also send you" (John 20:19-21).

Here for the first time, Jesus imparts his Spirit. Imagine being breathed upon and absorbing the "breath" of his risen, divine personality. This is no ordinary event! And the greeting of Shalom was not your everyday "Hello," though the word was familiar and could mean that, as "Aloha" does for Hawaiians. He came through doors closed by legitimate fear. The disciples were in danger only because of their association with him. When he manifested his now transformed, glorified wounds, they all entered a new dimension with regard to the situation. There was unshakeable joy. This Shalom was to convey "that peace which the world can neither give nor take away."

No doubt each person would have described a unique inner reaction. But their joy was communal. The first open recognition of the resurrection was to experience Jesus as the divine presence within a community. The Church (the word *ecclesia* means "the called together" or gathering) really begins now. This experience has become normal for Christians over the centuries: **Whenever two or three are gathered in my name, I will be in their midst** (Matthew 18:20).The Jewish quorum, the *minion*, was ten Sons of the Covenant; then the divine presence would constitute the synagogue. For Christians, the minion is as small as two, and these may be broadly inclusive - **neither Jew nor Greek, neither slave nor free, neither male nor female** (Galatians 3:28). The faithful experience of God was, from the beginning, corporate: **For you are all "sons of God"** (Females included!) **through faith in Christ Jesus. For as many of you as were baptized into Christ have put on Christ** (Galatians 3:26-27).

We all inhale and breathe an atmosphere impregnated with the Spirit of Shalom. Another whiff of the breath of Easter and we are given a work to do together. **The one who believes in me, the works that I do he will do also; and greater works he will do, because I go to my Father** (John 14:12). What works could be greater? Surely they are the same works in general, only infinitely more activities in time and space because of the geometrical increase in inspired persons. Our faith walk is a missionary journey with others in unity with the risen Jesus. Ours is essentially the same work Jesus had done in a single physical body. Now, free from physical constraint, he will live and act through many bodies. We must continually use this power to **abide in** the new life we have been given (John 15:4-11). This dimension of faith is corporate. Each of us must play our part in the breathing of the risen Christ's earthly body. We inhale his peace. And with the next breath the Spirit exhales into the world as we act out our faith. The Spirit incorporates us into a believing community. The faith journey is essentially corporate.

For journaling: *Have I thought of faith as an essentially private affair? What has been my experience of being part of a spirit-filled and directed community? Is the Holy Spirit's "fire in the fireplace" at my church? What is my place and work just now to be a faithful member of Christ's body the church?*

4. *Christ will bring us to the faith he requires.* Now Thomas, called the Twin, one of the twelve, was not with them when Jesus came. The other disciples therefore said to him, "We have seen the Lord." So he said to them, "Unless I see in his hands the print of the nails, and put my finger into the print of the nails, and put my hand into his side, I will not believe." And after eight days his disciples were again inside, and Thomas with them. Jesus came, the doors being shut, and stood in the midst, and said, "Peace to you!" Then he said to Thomas, "Reach your finger here, and look at my hands; and reach your hand here, and put it into my side. Do not be unbelieving, but believing." And Thomas answered and said to him, "My Lord and my God!" Jesus said to him, "Thomas, because you have seen me, you have believed. Blessed are those who have not seen and yet have believed" (John 20:24-29).

Individuals must be spiritually refurbished from time to time in order to be fruitful parts of the faith community. This passage is a great example of our need to know for ourselves, and of Jesus' desire to do whatever is required. He has come to bring Thomas' faith to the same level as the others. Thomas needed to see and touch the wounds, and came to an even fuller faith: **My Lord and my God!** We see and touch the Lord frequently in the veiled form of sacraments and other people, especially in meeting the needs of our neighbors. Yet we do not usually require special manifestations or religious phenomena to keep us moving faithfully along.

Faith, better than sight, is itself the essential human faculty that God has devised to keep us going into the fullness of life. Jesus attracts us to himself, to desire him. And then, meeting us in whatever condition of need, he provides just what is required to bring us to faith. He wants each person to **know his voice** and to **follow him** (John 10:3-4). It is the community's role to nurture the faith Jesus has quickened and drawn from each of us. This is why "faith development" is what healthy churches are about, and this is not just for the young. No one has fully arrived on the faith journey. God's grace does not pickle the faithful for eternity. He holds us in life and guides us at each stage of the journey into fullness of life.

For journaling: *"Am I willing to give as much of myself as I am able, to as much of God as I can understand?" (This is the evangelist Samuel Shoemaker's question for ongoing personal commitment.) What is my next step in the journey of faith? How will I take that step?*

MEDITATION:
MEETING THE RISEN SAVIOR- ON THE BEACH

Chapter 21 of John is like an appendix to the gospel. (Compare 20:30-31 and 21:25 to see the editorial seams have not been smoothed over.) In this set of post-resurrection narratives, there is a story of the disciples fishing together on the Sea of Tiberius just as in the old days; they weren't catching much. Jesus, at first not recognized, tells them from the shore what to do. After a magnificent catch and an astonishing recognition scene, Jesus invites them to share breakfast on the beach.

There is a place (in verse 4) from which we will slip around the edge of time and enter an eternal moment with Jesus: **When morning had now come, Jesus stood on the beach.**

Years ago the idea for the following meditation was given to me by a friend who had limited physical strength. So she developed a powerful habit of meditation to find inner resources to do the many things life required of her. It became a daily practice - really a way of life and not just a seasonal or sporadic spiritual exercise. Her way to encounter the risen Jesus was to slip between two verses of scripture into his abiding presence. The inspiration for this script came substantially from Oleen Misbach; but her idea was even simpler: just to be alone with Jesus on the beach in an eternal moment, to bask in his influence, like soaking up rays of sunshine.

(Gently lapping surf music accompanies the audio script on the enclosed CD.)

You are standing on top of a sand dune overlooking the sea, facing east. The sun rises over the water...Spend a few refreshing moments breathing the moist air, feeling the gentle breeze, and absorbing the increasing light of the new day...Offer a little prayer of thanks as you take off your shoes and get ready to go for a walk along the sandy shore...Just ahead are some stairs down to the beach. Deliberately descend and watch out for splinters. One step, two steps, three...Now feel your toes crunching the sand as you walk towards the smooth damp stretch of sand, the margin of land and water...Walking along, the light slowly intensifies into day, and you see up ahead a small boat some way offshore and on the beach a man looking out and saying something you can't hear... Gradually you come to recognize who it is –Jesus, the risen Savior. Drawing closer, you see he has a very unusual body, like nothing that has ever been. It has been born. It has lived. It has been crucified. And it has risen from death. It has ascended to the Father. It is human. It has marks on it and yet it is more than fully restored. ...And he walks slowly in your direction with a lightness that does not need the Earth and yet his feet still feel the crunch of the Galilean sand he has known since childhood...As you draw closer he notices you, but begins to start a small fire on which he will cook breakfast. His body exudes calm, like one who has finished almost everything. And he seems joyous that everything has been done well. He is whole, complete. He radiates love, yet with no desire to embrace. He seems to be in time, and also out of time. He is fully present. It is the same Jesus who comes to us in the Eucharist –in the bread and wine, the same person, full of calm and strength and joy...He extends his hand for you to sit down near him and of course you do that...Whatever energy flows from his presence makes you so comfortable you could just remain here, in and out of time...Stay here for a while. You may want to speak to him. He may speak to you, or not, just let it happen....

Now time resumes and he rises to gesture to the excited men drawing closer to shore in their over-loaded fishing boat. You rise too, and reverently move away. You walk back down the beach where your footprints from before still mark the path. Coming to the stairs, walk back up. Three... two... one. And you are back up on the dune. As you look back down the shore-line think about what you experienced in his presence by faith. And remember you can come back to this moment in and out of time whenever you want.

Discovering the Treasure Within

CHAPTER SEVEN

THE COUPLE
RELATIONSHIP & THE OTHER

A MATCH MADE IN HEAVEN

I never hoped to find a "girl of my dreams." It took a while to realize it, but then there she was. We had a few dates, out to dinner, dancing by the beach – but my life was very busy and full and I didn't realize what I'd found until I nearly lost her. One afternoon I called to cancel a dinner date because work was spilling over into the evening (not unusual for me).

On the phone she said, "I'm not a doll you can take down off the shelf when you feel like playing."

She said more, but this is all I remember. This confrontation was calm, no anger came through. Just the facts: this is the way it is. I knew I would either have to get really involved or forget it. Shocked and frightened, I knew myself to be out of control; I was about to give myself to another, a slippery feeling. It took a while, a few weeks, but I began to notice an attachment. I looked at her deeply and began to be attracted to more than her luminous skin. I would touch her cheek lightly and be fascinated. When we were apart for a day or so, my mind kept wandering back to her. It wasn't my mind exactly; my whole being vibrated like a tuning fork at the thought of her. I didn't really believe in romance. My sister had said I'd know when the real thing happened, and here it was. Well, not it, *she* happened to me, and I was hooked. I couldn't wait for evening when we could be together, if only for a short time. I wanted to freeze the way I felt and never change a thing, except to get married – that would be a way to have her all to myself forever. Actually, I felt offended to remember that the vow was "till death us do part." This was the most permanent, yes religious thing I'd ever done. Marriage was the way to keep this wonderful "in love" state of being forever.

After our wedding, six months or so later, the feeling of wonder at our

135

closeness had not gone away. But I did in fact grow enough accustomed to it to sort things out; being in love no longer took over all the corners of my mind. First, I remembered certain facts, like reading that those widowed in happy marriages were much more likely to remarry and enjoy the new relationship than those who felt relieved to be out of a painful coupling. Such widows, after all, liked being married; it isn't just the person of the spouse. And I also knew, at least rationally, that my bride could not be "the only one for me in the universe." Surely my being so totally in love had something to do with her being just the right age, available, compatible, and our looking forward to a family of our own. I did not feel these things, but I knew them.

In school, one of my favorite stories was The Little Prince, especially the episode where he left his tiny asteroid with its one beloved rose. He landed in a vast desert, it so happened, near a garden full of roses, each as lovely as "my rose." The Little Prince didn't fall for any of these beauties, but he grieved in deep disillusionment to learn that his love was not "unique in all the world." The wise fox taught him some lessons about love: it is not something you fall into and out of. A relationship that is real is not about a feeling.

The fox said it is about *taming*: "You are always responsible for what you have tamed."

And as the Little Prince experienced a bewildering disillusionment, so did I. Things were different now. Yes, I believed in love, but certainly not that romance was all there was to it, or even the most important part.

I went to my wife, fearful that she would think I loved her less than yesterday. I wept, afraid that our relationship would become too domesticated. She could no longer be the wild and crazy obsession at the heart of my life. It was an unmoored feeling, but there must be more to our life beyond this feeling. My beloved laughed, to my great surprise.

"How nice it will be to come down off that pedestal," she said. "No woman wants to be worshipped. It makes a person feel like an object, stuck in needing to be always the same for you. Now you can love me, at least sometimes, for what I am right then, whatever that may be. I couldn't be just what you thought I was. I was starting to feel trapped, enshrined. This may be a good thing for a movie starlet playing a role, but not for a real person."

This sobering truth was a moment of revelation for me. How selfish was my obsession! I had loved her for the way she made me feel. I still loved her romantically, and mostly she did bring me bright new feelings. But I knew there must be more; I had a strong sense that our actual marriage was just beginning. Now I began to make the acquaintance of the real woman I had married. Now we could really learn to be a couple.

++++++++++

Love, though we constantly read and talk about it, is an even bigger issue than we usually believe. Love is physical attraction, yes; love is a feeling of the heart and very strong, yes; but these things are not the major or even basic parts of love. A good, inclusive definition of most types of love, which we will expand and explore is: "Love is a decision which involves our feelings. Real love is acting in the best interests of the other."[11]

Let us consider love within the adult male/female couple relationship. By far the largest group of adults moves toward marriage, or is already living in a marriage. In our culture, although there is considerable variation, this is the fundamental expression of community. Not everyone gets married; not everyone is in a male/female primary relationship; but all of us are affected by the issues that arise from traditional marriage because it is so universally practiced. For the purposes of this presentation let us consider marriage between one man and one woman. By looking closely at a series of paintings, we will focus on several couple issues that are significant for successful marriage, both psychologically and spiritually. This section is not designed for individual journaling; but you and your spouse may want to write separate reflections, and later read what each one has written, then share further together about the insights and feelings that

---

[11]The definition used by World Wide Marriage Encounter is: "Love is not a feeling; it is what we do with our feelings. Love is a decision which involves our feelings."

come up. There are seven parts, each with paintings to mull over. The author suggests taking a week of focusing on exploring and strengthening your relationship together. Section Two is rich and could well be divided for an eighth day's reflection and sharing. (Full color copies of the images may be found on the accompanying CD.)

FOR REFLECTION AND DISCUSSION:
SEVEN ASPECTS OF LOVE

"Adam and Eve" (engraving), Albrecht Durer, 1504

I. THE PRIMAL COUPLE

The original biblical portrait of the couple, portrayed with strengths and weaknesses, is the primal pair, Adam and Eve (The Primal Couple Albrecht Durer, "Adam and Eve," lithograph, 1504). The Book of Genesis presents the spirituality of the couple at the outset; the couple is the primary unit of humanity. They are to be a reflection and thus a revelation of the Creator: **So God created man in his own image; in the image of God he created him; male and female he created them** (Genesis 1:27). The single unit of humanity is in fact the two: male and female. In depictions of Adam and Eve they are usually naked, sometimes behind a bush, transparently open to each other and not ashamed. Then as the story goes on, they have fig leaves indicating their fallen state. Still, their hiddenness was inner and spiritual, expressed outwardly, as inner matters always eventually are – the cover-up of a person who has hidden from a painful truth. The fig leaves seem quite ineffective, as if in the movie scene where the comedian is caught without pants in a hotel hallway; the embarrassing reality is apparent. Their nudity is not comical; but the cover-up is, even in the artist's elegant conception.

We recall this inner hiddenness was also expressed in blaming: **The woman gave me fruit of the tree, and I ate** (Genesis 3:12). Mutual recrimination is something all couples will recognize. It is so natural, under stress, for couples to locate a problem and project it on the other. This is a sure sign of the flawed nature we share. Those closest to us become our dumping place. There is definitely a sense of fear and shame lurking in human intimacy, however we choose to explain it. We easily build walls of defensiveness to hide from the beloved, and we cover ourselves to hide what we fear. But even in the midst of the primal tragedy, there is a less-frequently noticed sign of God's provision. At the end of the creation stories, just outside the Garden of Eden, the Lord provides something better than what the couple fashioned by their own artifice. The "fur coats" of Genesis 3:20 are clearly a sign of hope; blessing and grace prevail even as the painful consequences of the fall are played out. Clothing, in scripture, is often a symbol of *righteousness* - the restored relationship God is going to bring about, even in stories that seem to end in shame; we can persist in this ungraceful state, or we can move on through the power of confession and mutual forgiveness, to discovering and reflecting God's providence. This is the third scene that follows creation and fall: brokenness being restored in Christ. Couples are further clothed in the conventions of different times; this symbolizes the ways society conceives of family life.

Put on the Lord Jesus Christ, Paul advises, and when couples move beyond blame to forgiveness and reconciliation, the wedding garments are restored. True love must always include forgiveness at precisely the point where we would blame and reject. Successful marriage requires *mutual* forgiveness. It takes two. It also takes an understanding of true love ("the decision to act in the best interest of the other"). And it takes God: **We love because God first loved us** (I John 4:19). That love always offers forgiveness.

For Reflection and Sharing: Couple counselors often note the time it takes early in therapy for couples to take responsibility for their anger, and to express it without projecting all the blame on the spouse. Healing and behavior change only begin at this point. What has been your experience with blaming things on each other? Have you been able to give and receive forgiveness from each other (and God) from time to time? Discuss examples, clear the air, and reach out to each other in loving forgiveness. And then move on.

II. TWO MISMATCHES

This is John William Waterhouse's Victorian English take on a relationship that could never go anywhere, not even to a divorce court. "Echo and Narcissus" are doomed from the start. He is so cursed by fate (Nemesis) that he cannot relate to another, just his own reflection. She is so obsessed with him that she, also cursed, can only repeat phrases of what he has said. Overall, these are not ingredients of good communication. The story of the fair but forlorn nymph and the son of a nymph and a river god have been the subject of poems from Ovid to Keats. In various guises they appear in novels and movies. Not so long ago Hollywood featured the lovely Nicole Kidman in "To Die For," the tale of a weather girl aspiring to become a news anchor. The character is so obsessed with her career that she charms a young man to help murder the husband who stands in her path to self-fulfillment. Though psychological researchers say less than 1% of the population can be diagnosed with Narcissistic Personality Disorder, which this character typifies, the tendency to be self absorbed and/or desperately obsessed resonates with us all; hence the recurring interest in this ancient scenario.

The contemporary media-dominated culture feeds these immature, me-first impulses. The following is from a reflection posted in 2010 on the popular blog, "The Last Psychiatrist:"

> *"Narcissism doesn't mean you think you're the greatest person on earth, but rather that all things in the world are relevant only as they impact you...Being on YouTube, having a blog, social networking...all these things are self-validating, they allow the illusion that is so important to narcissists: that we are the main characters in a movie...that everyone around us is supporting cast: the funny friend, the crazy ex, the neurotic mother, the egotistical date, etc. This makes reminders of our insignificance even more infuriating."*[12]

For Reflection and Sharing: The genius of Christianity, its transforming power, is in focusing on the other. We find life by laying it down in the best interest of others. This is especially so in intimate relationships. Two questions should recur:

1. What have I done in your best interest today?
2. How have I experienced the impulse to self-centeredness today?

Reflect, and share.

++++++++++

Sometimes mismatches are formalized and celebrated. There is available on the internet a painting by Stanley Spencer, known for New Testament scenes set in his hometown in England. His "Self-Portrait with Patricia Preece" 1936, reveals a couple that can never form anything but a toxic relationship. Their marriage was never consummated. Though together and totally exposed to each other, they are single. Like the two single beds that have been pushed together, these two may be close, but they will not connect. Stanley Spencer paints with great realism the experience he could not see, even with his glasses on. Patricia Preece

---

[12] See: http//www.thelastpsychiatrist.com

convinced him to divorce his wife Hilda and to marry her, after deeding the house to her. He continued to write daily letters to Hilda. Sister Wendy Beckett, herself a single person, offers insightful commentary in a short gallery tour posted on YouTube:

> *"The general impression I perceive is vaguely comic: a funny little man with a scraggly neck...gazing vacantly past, not even at, this siren whom he feels is so seductive but who strikes us as so heavily unattractive... At some level Stanley knows that they can never be united: his art knows it though he himself does not. The very contrasts of their body colors and her obvious lack of interest make this clear. She is not spread out for his delectation; she is acting as though he was not there, which, for her, he clearly never was. He looks not at her but into emptiness, with a set, bewildered, unhappy expression, yet he insists on painting them as a pair."*[13]

This second picture of a mismatch, and the romantic episode that led to it, points to the psychological relationship that underlies coupling. Sometimes romantic attraction can develop to mutual satisfaction and sometimes not. Carl Jung, in describing the inner archetypes, spoke of the woman in the man and the corresponding man within each woman. These powerful inner images, patterns of energy basic to the brain, are shaped and developed in large part by internalizing one's experience of the opposite sex parent (or parent figure). Thus, *falling in love* – anything from a crush to an obsession, to attraction to another of a certain type – is a projection of this inner image (*animus or anima*) onto a real person. If both are "in love" there is a certain mutual attraction. There is always, of course, a degree of mismatching of the image and reality. There is also mismatching between the *anima* projection of the man and the *animus* of the woman: the likelihood of "animosity" developing from time to time is very great. Unless the relationship is inherently toxic (falling in love with a series of

---

[13] Sister Wendy Beckett, <u>Odyssey: A Journey of Artistic Discovery,</u> 1993, page 24. This is also posted on YouTube as a short lecture.

addicted persons, for example), it is part of the maturing process to work through these animosities. For this we need a therapeutic communication technique (and often, a therapist) that involves four processes:

1. Separating from the "beloved" enough to see the projection that draws us close, but then hits a barrier. The most important guideline for doing this is to avoid blaming the other for the way we feel: not "You make me feel...," but "When this happens, I feel..."

2. Removing judgment from feelings. The inner emotional self is morally neutral. We may not always *like* feeling a certain way, but it is important to accept and look at whatever the feeling is, without blame or rejection. Only then is it possible to let go of it or to communicate the feeling to another.

3. Then expanding. As couples mature, the *animus/anima* projection that drew and bonded them early on should become less central to their love: a bridge to the other rather than a magnet.

4. Lifelong development. It is helpful to understand that the *oneness* that couples expect to feel and need to develop fully is not static. As many psychologists have pointed out, the emotional bond of love between the couple cycles and recycles through the process:

- *Romance - animus/anima* projection
- *Disillusionment* - often accompanied by animosity, despair, bitterness, and the like
- *Joy* - a deeper, but always temporary sense of union and mutual satisfaction

When this complex process is understood and accepted, it is possible to manage the negative transitional feelings more smoothly and efficiently, without fear or the sensation of "spinning our wheels." Deeper self-giving and receiving from the other then builds a strong new phase in the relationship.

Healthy couples have a broad range of mutually satisfying behaviors and remain flexible as life's changes come along. The relationship should be something both people would like "to come home to" – a domestic arrangement grounded in profound friendship will be able to fulfill the vows to "love, honor, and cherish" for a lifetime. Ideally each partner will declare his feelings, needs and perceptions, but not judgments. And then they will negotiate a solution in behalf of their relationship.

For Reflection and Sharing: Try this technique: Write about a mutually agreed problem area. Describe in detail your perception of the situation, your thoughts and feelings about it, and what you are willing and able to do to make changes. Share what you have written and discuss it.

Of course, emotionally sensitive and repetitive issues are seldom clear and simple. Two conditions common to all couple relationships should be kept in mind with strategies to overcome them. Marital unity ranges between the extremes of fusion and fighting. The next two familiar paintings portray these states beautifully; though they represent parts of the cycle, they are not good places to get stuck.

III. THE FUSED COUPLE

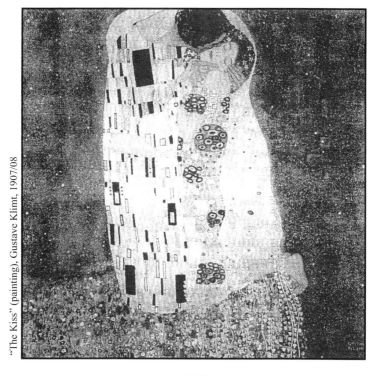

"The Kiss" (painting), Gustave Klimt, 1907/08

145

"The Kiss" is an ecstatic painting meant to represent erotic unity, but it is also an emotional unity that is so wonderfully expressed. The psychological boundaries have nearly disappeared. The gold communicates the spiritual feeling of being "one flesh:" more one than two separate people. And the gold indicates the religious quality of this experience. But like most glorious feelings that we would like to stop time to enshrine, the orgasmic moment has a dark side; without boundaries that give a clear sense of where *I* begin and ***the other*** takes over. Sometimes marital therapists encounter an emotionally *fused* couple, where it seems two people make up only one whole person. The ecstatic feeling of unity, when it is prolonged, (when one loses self to swim in a transcendent sea of being, flecked by notes of color) means that one person has what the other lacks and no longer needs to develop further. For example, he *thinks* and she *feels*; or when one person dominates the other, experiencing either the power or vulnerability of the other. This is an unhealthy situation. A satisfying, long-term couple relationship has passion and ecstatic moments, but there is also an emotional distinctness that keeps the personalities from blurring; there is room for both to grow. In a healthy relationship each person maintains the *solitude* of singleness; and this is what they offer to each other, sexually and in all other ways as well. There is no "giving up" or "giving in" to the other, just joyful "giving to" each other (These are phrases from the Marriage Encounter Weekend).

For Reflection and Discussion: In what areas do we need to find a healthy spaciousness right now? Where do we need to bend to each other in compromise? Are there any habitual communication "attitudes" we should begin to let go for the sake of our relationship? Reflect and share.

IV. THE FIGHTING COUPLE

"The Conversation" (painting). Henri Matisse, 1908-1912

In sharp contrast to the Klimt picture, another famous modern painting portrays too much distance; it exemplifies fighting, the other extreme from fusion. Just as fusion, however, is not the essence of intimate union, neither should fighting need to indicate the breaking of a healthy union. All couples fight, but they can also reconcile. And they can fight fairly and with skill, not to hurt each other but for the greater good of their relationship. This painting presents a couple too far apart. The intervening window contrasts, and the grill distilling the conversational content says "Non" in wrought iron; these speak volumes about how far they feel themselves to be from each other at this moment. They have conspicuous ears, yet they cannot hear each other. Even though they are close enough to talk, there is a feeling of abysmal distance; their feelings seem to have drained out into the lovely garden. Though face to face, they have taken positions that put them on different levels (standing and sitting). Is he talking down to her? He appears rigid, straight and unbending like the lines in his suit. She is stuck seated bulkily in the cold blue color of the wall. Is this the emotional atmosphere in which their relationship takes place? And she is clothed in the same black as the stiff but feminine curves of the wrought iron. What a contrast to the floating, touching, glowing colors of **"The Kiss."**

However, if they will move out of these cold, frozen attitudes, there is hope. It appears in the green of her scarf which draws the eye to the bright loveliness of the garden. The lighter blue and white of his clothing are reflected in the flowing beauty of the flower beds, and the tree trunk outside the window is stiff but supporting a puff of leaves. Will they move towards each other just a little? Whoever can change his or her attitude first will begin to turn the argument into dialogue. He stiffly prefers being right to being one with her; she stubbornly leans back into her resistance. Can they look past their disagreement instead of solving it? Will they move beyond the negative into the soul garden, the relationship they share together?

For Reflection and Sharing: How do we usually get through an argument? Take an agreed example from the past and notice the process and not the content: what started it (both sides)? Then what happened? How did we fuel the fight? How did we resolve it?

Do we have an agreed way to resolve conflicts when they arise? (We need to be generally close enough to feel and nurture the respect and mutuality of our friendship.) How can we better affirm each other or reach out to get the conversation going with renewed hope?

V. FROM INSTITUTION TO SACRAMENT IN MARRIAGE

"The Arnolfini Marriage" (painting), Jan Van Eyck, 1422

This renowned painting illustrates some things about the sacrament of marriage. Here two prosperous, middle class persons are making vows publicly witnessed by the painter and another reflected in the convex mirror at the focal point of the picture. The painter has loaded the portrait with symbolism. The Arnolfinis wear their finery – clothing symbolizing the best and highest offering, the culture and style of their relationship, as good a symbol of couple unity as nakedness before each other. The man receives her lightly offered hand, and his other hand, raised in a gesture of blessing, corresponds to her hand lightly resting on her womb in expectation of a fruitful union. (Scholars say pregnancy is not the issue.) The wedding bed is decked in red, symbolic of passion, but also of the Holy Spirit. The pair of Flemish clogs and the dog point to the holiness of the domestic and ordinary, for those who have eyes to see it. Recall the story of Moses who was instructed to remove his shoes in the presence of the burning bush that was not consumed – a sign of God's self-revelation (Exodus 3:5). And also, more obscurely but literally, notice the giving of a sandal recalling an ancient sign of redemption in marriage. Ruth's *go'el* (savior) was Boaz (Ruth 4:7-11) according to ancient Hebrew custom; the sandal seals the redemptive act. There is a redemptive character in the life of Holy Matrimony. In our day, when so many marriages are ending in divorce, this character needs to be recognized and widely celebrated.

The little lap dog also represents domestic life – *nature* structured in such a way that the animal tendencies may be tamed and civilized. (How much of holy parenting involves bringing civility and structure to the impulsive animal nature, shaping and forming a family?) It is the deep spirituality of couple unity that, given its due, will exalt us and allow us to realize our human potential for goodness and fulfillment: that is, holiness. Here is portrayed the potential of marriage for elevating the social institution to manifest its sacramental character. Holy Matrimony is not just a liturgical form or civil institution; it is an outward and visible sign of the love of God, a continuation of the incarnation of the Word.

Notice the mirror on the wall between the man and woman. The painter has placed it there to indicate human nature is designed to reflect God's glory.

This mirror is framed with ten miniatures illustrating the redemptive life of Christ. Look carefully at the close-up detail (see next page) to see the familiar scenes of the passion story. (These details are obscure even in the original painting which is not large.) It is this transforming life that marriage, spiritually conceived, is meant to reflect and reveal- the *image of God*. When the man and woman look into the mirror, they should see themselves surrounded by the sacrificial love of Christ, as a reminder that they are to lay down their lives for each other. The couple cannot be expected to reflect God's omnipotence or omniscience, but only God's love. **We love, because he first loved us** (I John 4:19). Sustained by God's love, human love can become a "means of grace." Note the biblical theme of the

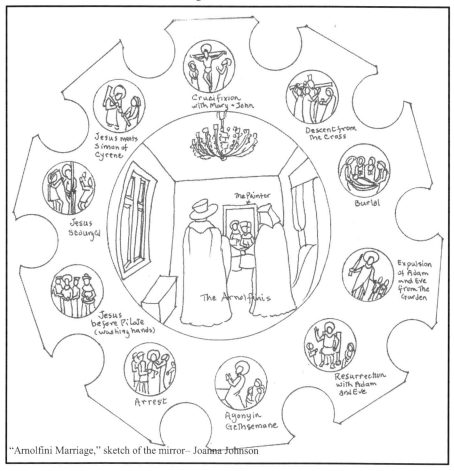

"Arnolfini Marriage," sketch of the mirror– Joanna Johnson

correspondence of the relationship of wife and husband to that of Christ and the Church. This *mystery* or sacramental character of married love is described in Ephesians 5: 30-33.

Where is God in this painting? Certainly it is not a "church wedding." (Art historians no longer see this painting as a betrothal or a certification of the Arnolfini's marriage.) Still, God is plainly represented. In the red color of the marriage bed, the Spirit may symbolically support and cover them; and there is the sacred story of Christ surrounding the mirror. There is further, to round out the Trinititarian symbolism with the most painterly clarity, the image of light burning in the single candle in the brass chandelier and streaming through the clear window to the left that bathes everything in the room in the light of day. The light symbol may represent many ideas, but certainly it emphasizes this couple's intent to live in the unity of marriage, rather than as single individuals. This all takes place in broad daylight, for all to witness. The reality that the painter celebrated with every brush stroke is God's involvement with the couple's everyday life. This painting, even centuries later, reminds couples that their divinely illuminated daily life can be a "Celebration of Holy Matrimony," not just on the wedding day.

For Reflection and Discussion: In what specific ways do we represent and reflect God in our marriage?

When has your love for me been especially sacrificial?

VI. THE HEROIC COUPLE

"Hercules and Deianira" (painting), Jan Gossart (Mabuse), 1517

We associate the legendary Hercules with heroic action. As super-hero of the ancient world, he is the archetypal image of masculine physical strength. In this 16th century painting the hero is with his wife Deianeira. It seems to present the psychological ideal in a physical image. Lest we be intimidated by the idealized physicality, the story of this pair reveals that they have their flaws, as do we all. There are no perfect couples, though ideals are there to be models. Hercules won his wife in battle with a rapist who, with his last gasp of malicious energy, cursed the hero by whispering a message of doom in Deianeira's ear. She was to dip the corner of a cloak in his blood and use it to bring power to Hercules in time of need. Deianeira, much later, in fact at the end of the love story, wraps her wounded husband in the garment which, as we might guess, is poisoned. Hercules' physical strength, invulnerable in many tests, has a limit like all mortals. She too has limits, just an ordinary girl at heart, like the heroines of Wagnerian operas. Deianeira gullibly trusted the "blessing" of her attacker, treasuring in her heart what turned out to be a curse like a poisonous snake, waiting for provocation. So, as we look at this heroic couple, we warm to them as ideal but, like the rest of us, flawed and vulnerable. It is all portrayed: a balance, not precisely *animus/anima,* which are really two parts of one person. Here we have two emotionally whole, complete persons, joined in a unity of mutual respect and poised strength. They are seated on a bench enclosed within the shelter of a tomb-like niche. The sculpture in relief suggests scenes of battle, the victories of the hero in hand-to-hand combat and various trials. He is the embodiment of the same tough warrior we see in countless variations in action-adventure movies, detective stories, and legends of knights inspired to valor by the maiden in the castle back home. But we seldom see this natural ideal so simply put as in Gossaert's painting. Notice the unity symbolized, not in passionate desire, but in their intertwined legs. They are not struggling as wrestlers would, grappling for advantage. There is no competition between these warriors; instead there is a powerful poise, a relationship depicted as warmly as flesh, as enduring as the classical niche in which they might be preserved forever. This living unity is more than a peaceful moment in the midst of struggling action and eventual death. They represent the maturity and wholeness of couple love: an ideal seldom attained, hence truly heroic, as **those who have come through the great ordeal** (Revelation 7:14). They will not know defeat even in death.

The secret of this powerful classical marriage is revealed in three ways we might well emulate. Like Adam and Eve before the Fall, they are unashamedly naked; both have discarded the normally needed defenses in male and female interaction. He rests his terrible war club on the ground. She holds but does not wear her lavender gown with a gold border. They have not discarded these symbols with which they present themselves to others. Their intimacy is not a pre-fall innocence; strong enough, not naïvely, they lay aside their defenses for the eternal moment of their love. It is a wonderful image of that emotional openness that strong marriages all have – a potent ideal of struggle transcendent and victorious.

Notice also the strength with which they hold each other. Each draws the other close in a different way, and there is a closeness that is somehow not too close. This attitude reflects the wholeness of emotional maturity; they are beyond the obsessions and brokenness of youth and the neuroses of the immature. (Compare with the Spencer painting- a unity of disconnect). This is an image of love and support; they are at each other's side, equals confirming the strength of the other.

Finally, they are looking into each other's eyes, and into each other's souls. Like Narcissus looking for a reflection of himself, she looks for what he sees; he looks beyond but without leaving Deianeira out of the picture. These two may be tragically flawed, with tough times to come, but it doesn't take a lot of insight to recognize the eternal dimension in the heroic attitude of what they see together. This is a bold image of the couple archetype.

For Reflection and Discussion: What are we like when our relationship is at its best? What are our strengths as a couple? What can we do to nurture this goodness in order to grow toward greatness?

VII. THE SPIRITUAL CALLING OF MARRIAGE

"The Embrace of St. Anne and St. Joachim" (etching), Lucas van Leydan, 1520

The spiritual dimension of marriage blossoms when a couple allows what God would do with their marriage to become paramount. An example of such a mature relationship is Joachim and Anne, the parents of Mary the mother of Jesus. They mirror Abraham and Sarah, also surprisingly fruitful in old age, whose child brought a profound blessing to the world. Maybe these couples need to be older to represent the completion of those earlier aspects of most marriages: finding a compatible lifestyle, raising a family and managing careers. This 16th Century etching focuses attention with intense purity on the essence of married spirituality: living together wholly for God. When this happens, a couple's family history becomes part of the story of God's redeeming work. Of course, children are but one example of fruitfulness for God.

The contemporary icon on the CD also represents a meeting that demonstrates the couple's complete unity with God's purpose for them. Known as "The Embrace," this is the pre-eminent model of a normal married couple, unique in the canon of traditional icons. In the apocryphal back-story (from the "Proto-Evangelion of James") Mary's parents have both had angelic encounters, in different locations, revealing that they should have a special child. Now they meet in a hug of recognition that is deeply emotional as well as spiritual. The two trees to the right of their home may remind us of consecrated nature, the Tree of Life, even of Baucis and Philemon, the legendary couple blessed for their hospitality. The Lucas van Leyden etching also is bushy with suggestive foliage. Joachim and Anne come from different directions, with differing points of view, as do all couples. There is movement, yet the bodies "cheek to cheek" seem to float above a raised platform in a spiritual plane. Joachim's feet barely touch ground; Anne's cloak opens to him with a flourish of passion. Their outer cloaks glow with the same festive red; but their inner garments are in sharp contrast—his blue, hers green. They bend towards one another, submitting to each other in love. Note, there is no inequality or domination in their postures. With great modesty they reveal complete intimacy in a moment of transcendent gratitude that reminds one of those breath-taking love duets at the climax of hundreds of musical dramas: *Yes! This is it!* **This at last is bone of my bones and flesh of my flesh** (Genesis 2:23). Resonating with the archetype, once again a human couple is striking the original match.

For Reflection and Discussion: Looking back upon our life together, what are some moments which stir in me the feeling of gratitude? When have I experienced gratitude about us recently?... Write journal reflections on these questions and share your responses.

Another question: What do I think God might have in mind for us as a couple just now? Discuss further: How could we cooperate? Then holding hands, pray together in simple informal words.

+++++++++++

For those who have enjoyed these reflections, the author offers three alternatives for continuing:

If you have a trusted pastor, make an appointment to discuss how you might strengthen your relationship. Most clergy are trained in this practice and rely on strong marriages to build the larger Christian community. If there seem to be ongoing conflicts or nagging issues, the pastor will personally refer you to a local counselor who specializes in therapy for couples, generally short-term and affordable.

Many pastors are trained in a widely used program known as Prepare/ Enrich, from the University of Minnesota. This will involve taking a well-researched inventory to discover your strengths and growth areas as a couple. There is a version for effective pre-marital preparation, but also a version for enrichment which can be presented with a small group of couples who want to grow and strengthen their relationships in the face of all the stresses of our culture.

For those who see themselves having a good (not perfect!) marriage – which means they plan to stay together and have a deep commitment to their marriage and family life - the best available enrichment activity is to attend a Marriage Encounter Weekend. This is an intensive, private time to work on deep communication with a strong sacramental perspective. Information and local contacts are available on the web at www.wwme.org.

CHAPTER EIGHT

THE ELDER
MATURITY & HOMECOMING

THE ANCIENT OF DAYS

This is not just any walk in the woods; it is a pilgrimage to the oldest living things on earth. Even the most hardened logger would walk reverently in the hush of Redwood National Park. I began my walk at the Dolason Prairie Trail head. Plodding toward the "Garden of the Giants," my imagination conjured childlike anticipation. Maybe it would be personal and eerie, like spending the night among the walking trees Tolkien described; but the adult in me turned from that image. It's much harder to personalize the vegetable kingdom than our nearer neighbors, the dogs and cats, lambs, lions and dolphins. Another remembered image evoked primal feelings: it will be like walking through the Joyce Kilmer Forest in North Carolina, the only remaining virgin forest in America's east. But the adult chimes in again, reminding me of the trail guide: "Of the 2,000,000 acres of redwood forest the California 49ers found only 4% remains." What I will see is not untouched; maybe something has to be scarce in the commercial world in order to seem worth saving, now too valuable to harvest for lumber.

The "Tall Trees Grove" was where I headed with mixed feelings of anticipation- not to worship, or picket, or mythologize the *Sequoia sempervirens*; my plan was to enjoy the existence of trees, the oldest of which broke from its seed before the birth of Jesus. How could even a cynic fail to be moved by the presence of living creatures so old?

I was not disappointed. Tears flowed as I gradually moved among the planet's most ancient trees, as close as anything has come to immortality. In the grove beneath the canopy, the afternoon sunlight is filtered; the guidebook calls it "a green-filtered undersea radiance!"[14] –in a phrase which aptly describes the holy hush of light. I sat for a while to absorb the quiet splendor through all my senses. Looking up the house-sized trunk, the ridged and rutted gray bark, I'm surprised to think of the most wrinkled old people I've known.

At about 50ft up, the lowest branches spread a green roof that shelters myriad creatures in a constantly dripping ecosystem. The guide was right, "Observing hurts the neck from craning to see the crown, and the mind from trying to grasp the monumentality, and near immortality, of this life form." Living for hundreds of years, no two trees are alike; each one would have a story slowly unfolded through long cycles of more or less rain, through countless storms and microbial invasions and assaults of insects.

In this "twinkling of an eye" there are human visitors, like me. Let me speak for the voiceless ones who seem unimpressed: "Who are these ephemera that we should be mindful of them?"

Nurturing a philosophical sense of awe toward ancient earth, their survivor wisdom towered around me. I walked back to the trailhead through younger forests and meadows of short-lived wildflowers and grasses. *Why is it*, I thought, *babies look pretty much alike, as do many movie actors and models; and we admire their young faces and covet their smooth skin? Yet the aged, wrinkled like a redwood, with unique and distinctive lines of experience, do not represent our human aspirations, though they embody the destiny of everyone who lives long enough. Why is it so hard to appreciate and lift up the natural beauty of the very old?*

For Reflection and Journaling: In the psychological dimension, we move gladly toward **wholeness.** This process we considered previously in the adult phase; now consider the ultimate dynamics of becoming whole. There are several aspects to human fulfillment and maturity; certainly two of them are **being fully tamed**, and **being well-balanced.**

1. **Taming** is a concept taken from Antoine de St. Exupery's modern parable The Little Prince. This story illustrates the process by which persons may come truly and fully to know each other both because of and in spite of radical differences. In a state of lonely frustration the boy who is

---

[14]Details & quotes are from Kenneth Brower, "Into the Garden of the Giants," National Geographic Traveler, July/Aug. 2005.

the story's hero, wants to play with a fox whose path has crossed his own. The boy wants distraction. The fox wisely rejects his offer of friendship. He says, "I am not tamed." The fox defines this for the puzzled extra-terrestrial boy as "an act too often neglected, meaning *to establish ties*." The dissimilarity between boy and fox is intriguing, especially as it speaks to the other-ness problem: across cultures, between the sexes, and between God and creation- what the Danish theologian Soren Kierkegaard famously called "the infinite qualitative distinction." Given the difference between a lonely boy and the wild fox, certain regular rituals will be required in order to establish a mutually beneficial relationship. The fox calls this "taming."

This suggestive concept is a metaphor about establishing genuinely mature relationships. For it is not just by searching out such qualities as likeness, or common interest, or opposites attracting, that one comes truly to know persons. It is by building trust – **taming**. And the need for this does not come initially from a sense of incompleteness. It comes from disillusionment and the failure of life to be sufficiently meaningful. According to the fox, taming begins by deciding to take time for a relationship, and then grows into friendship by patiently drawing closer, not with words, but by "sitting a little closer every day." This needs a dependable routine of "proper rites." And with taming goes an ethical bond of mutual accountability: *"Men have forgotten this truth," said the fox, "but you must not forget it. You become responsible forever for what you have tamed."*

How clearly this reflects the personal fellowship that can come to maturity between God who is *wholly* other, and the creation, including us! When taming occurs, there comes about an inter-penetration of personality without confusion or absorption. This is the essence of personal knowledge. It is the thought of such a joyful outcome that eventually inspires the fox to risk knowing this strange boy, who is so like his natural enemy, the hunter, and who comes to him curiously from a planet that has neither hunters nor chickens. In a lyrical monologue,[15] St. Exupery's fox describes the possibility of expanded awareness and vitality, just before inviting the

---

[15] Antoine de St. Exupery, The Little Prince, Harcourt, Brace, Jovanovich, Inc. NY, 1971, page 83

strange little prince into a *taming* relationship:

> *"My life is very monotonous," he said. "I hunt chickens; men hunt me. All the chickens are just alike, and all the men are just alike. And, in consequence, I am a little bored. But if you tame me, it will be as if the sun came to shine on my life. I shall know the sound of a step that will be different from all the others. Other steps send me scurrying back underneath the ground. Yours will call me, like music, out of my burrow. And then look: you see the grain fields down yonder? I do not eat bread. Wheat is of no use to me. The wheat fields have nothing to say to me. And that is sad. But you have hair that is the color of gold. Think how wonderful that will be when you have tamed me! The grain, which is also golden, will bring me back the thought of you. And I shall love to listen to the wind in the wheat..."*
>
> *The fox gazed at the little prince for a long time.*
>
> *"Please tame me," he said.*
>
> *"I want to very much," the little prince replied. "But I have not much time. I have friends to discover, and a great many things to understand."*
>
> *"One only understands the things that one tames," said the fox...*

And so **Taming** is a lifelong occupation.

St. Paul reminds us that there is even a cosmic dimension to taming: **Up till now the whole universe groans in the pains of childbirth.** (Romans 8: 22). The prophet Isaiah spoke of the messianic kingdom when **the lion will lie down with the lamb.** We are reminded of the promise of paradise restored, a peaceable kingdom, where the red thread of the Spirit will ultimately displace the "rule of tooth and claw."

2. **Balance**, the other key aspect of maturity, manifests the gift of God's "Shalom." This is a dynamic balance, moving and bending with the Spirit, like riding a bicycle. But to maintain the balance of peace, and to internalize

and express peace takes a lifetime of attentive practice. Think of the contrast between toddlers learning to walk, and the traditional Chinese lifetime spiritual practice of Tai Chi, with its ever-deepening lessons about balance, flexibility and presence. Human maturation does not peak shortly after puberty. It takes a lifetime of practice and prayer: "Teach me to care, and not to care. Teach me to be still." (T.S. Eliot, Four Quartets.)

Journaling Question: *What about me threatens to get old without growing up? What do I want to do about this?*

In the moral plane, maturity aims for another kind of wholeness: **fruitfulness** and **integrity.** When a person has come alive in the Spirit, there is an ongoing fruitfulness that should be evident. This "crop" is a product of healthy spirituality; it cannot be forced or developed with "willpower." A middle-aged friend was poking with his lawn rake at the oak leaves clinging to his trees in late fall. He wanted to finish raking, get the job done for the year. It was a little embarrassing when his wife laughed and reminded him, "Oak leaves don't fall all at once; it's futile to beat the branches. This inconvenience is the price of living on Oak Street." Moral maturity also requires patience. St. Paul wrote in several places of the effect of the spiritual life overcoming the merely human (and even subhuman) nature we all share. **The fruit of the Spirit is** (nine-fold): **love, joy, peace, patience, gentleness, kindness, faithfulness, goodness, and self-control** (Galatians 5: 22-23).

The same friend who tried to speed up the fall cleanup also noticed that these ethical fruits are likely to grow as successive crops, like roses that bloom several times a season, producing at last the exquisite "last rose of summer." In the development of spiritual fruit the first crop is often a heartfelt desire to **love,** along with **joy and peace.** Then something bad happens or someone plucks off the fruit, leaving a desperate sense of loss and grief, but making way for the next crop of **patience, gentleness and kindness.** Patience is long-suffering, the dark part of waiting; only the beloved who has given love will have the strength required to mute anger and forgive, to become patient, to practice being gentle and to perform acts of kindness. After these fruits ripen and are plucked, **faithfulness and**

goodness are able to develop as a result of growing maturity, still more beautiful than autumn roses. And last of all emerges **self-control** which we would all like to produce early on; but only the spiritually maturing reveal seasoned virtue. In a dry season, the faithful ones whom the Lord sustains **will not be anxious and will remain fruitful.** (Jeremiah 17: 18).

Journaling Question: *What kind of ethical fruit are you producing these days? Have you tended the current crop through prayer, asking for the nutrients that can make your life full of fruit?*

+++++++++++

According to Jung, the spiritual goal of maturity is **individuation.** By this he meant that by gradually separating from automatic, instinctive and culturally based behavior, we will become more and more a unique being. Thus coming to full maturity involves the central exercise of choice with the freedom we have. The very young grow almost naturally; with good nutrition, babies will become toddlers. Others supply the necessary conditions and the body just grows. Even after puberty, the change is not simply a choice, though ethics and wise use of personal freedom require effort. The 20th century English evangelist Bryan Greene told of a young girl who had been raised by atheists and therefore couldn't trust or believe in God.

"You can't convince me that there is a God or that God cares."

"I know this," he responded to her," but I also know that eventually life will break you and you will know your need for God. Come, talk to me then."

Ten years later he got a call from the same young woman who asked, "Do you remember me and what you said to me? Well, you were right. May I come and talk with you?"

As adults age, growth continues, but choices become more prominent in coming to maturity.

Journaling Question: *Think of a time when you have chosen to grow as a person. What was the process like, and its outcome? ...How are you* *choosing to grow now? What part does God seem to contribute to the process?*

SCRIPTURE REFLECTION & JOURNALING: I CORINTHIANS 15: THE HUMAN BODY - AGING & TRANSCENDENCE

The deterioration of the mature physical body through infirmity and age is an inescapable fact of human life. But it is not the last word. Perhaps we can move towards a more spiritual approach to the body in order to counteract the influence of today's "youth cult."St. Paul wrote: **The first Adam became a living being; the last Adam became a life-giving spirit. However, the spirit is not first, but the natural, and afterward the spiritual.** (I Corinthians 15: 45-46).

A TRIBUTE TO LAUREN

Lauren was a woman whose lifespan was cut short by an incurable blood cancer. She lived a difficult life successfully because she matured early. Although Carl Jung thought real spiritual development could only begin at about age 50, Lauren lived fully and died shortly after her 49th birthday.

Her mother had been "wild" and drank heavily, but she had the freedom that comes with lavish financial resources. Even as an elderly woman, she would call a cab after the nurse left for the day, to take her to a local watering hole. Some years back, Lauren received a phone call from a ship off the coast of Italy, to come and pick up her mother at the next port of call; she was too drunk, disruptive and difficult to complete the cruise. Lauren was a highly developed "caretaker" – more mature than her mother, even as a young woman. This family role influenced her life story for better and worse. Her ability (and need) to be in charge steered her through several marriages, but she always managed to come out on top. She was also a woman of faith, learning early in the midst of a complex and broken family, that God was close and could be trusted even when no one else could be. In her late forties she met a man with his own story of failures in love; they married in lavish style with a theme she had always cherished-butterflies. After the reception there was a special release of newly-hatched butterflies to crown the occasion. Alas, in short order the groom, who had learned to prefer solitude as his own way of coping, decided he no longer loved Lauren; indeed, he didn't like to be around her, so he left the marriage. Preparing once again to deal with a disastrous turn of events that she was accustomed to managing, she channeled her hurt and anger into positive recovery and into being a good friend to many. Then she developed a debilitating illness which she also managed with skill, equanimity and grace. Having presided at her wedding, I was the one Lauren called when her doctor told her the time was short and she should get her affairs in order.

Trusting herself to the care of a few good friends, she decided to live the last weeks of her life as fully as possible. She organized all the details, even of her funeral, so that her friends would be at ease with it all. Lauren made peace with family members, cared for her young adult son, and forgave her ex-husband. I came to know her well and to admire one who, having lived a painful life now about to end seemed to mature spiritually without bitterness and with an unshakeable will to persevere faithfully. Her home that she refused to leave was tastefully furnished, especially with butterfly motifs of every type imaginable. Because of a family history of substance abuse, she used very little of the hospice-administered morphine and so remained lucid in her last days. Lauren had always been trim and stunningly beautiful; now as her jaundiced skin began to bloat and waste visibly, she laughed and said,

"To think I always prided myself on my concave stomach."

As the end approached, I told Lauren to call me anytime she wanted for any reason.

Two weeks before she died, she outlined her funeral plan and discussed cremation; could she have a cross to wear that would accompany her body? On the day of her death she called me to ask for Holy Communion with a few friends. When I arrived a woman said,

"She's been seeing angels all around."

To which Lauren remarked with simple honesty, "No they weren't; I just thought they were."

When time came for her to receive communion, I placed a piece of the Host on her tongue and moistened her mouth with a sip of water. In a weak voice, but very clearly, as I knelt close to her, she said, "I love you Jesus. Praise and glory be to God."

As I spread her ashes on the sea, I reflected on Lauren, butterflies, and her spiritual maturity. Hers was a life cut short, but complete. She was ready to transcend this life for a better one.

Journaling Question: *There is much "lost and found" in a lifetime. What does your "body image" mean to you at this time? What are your feelings about living with the aging process? What have your mini death and resurrection experiences been like? Do you agree that we never want to go backwards in life or to relive a certain period? Examine this idea for yourself and your feelings about reviewing your own life story.*

SCRIPTURE REFLECTION & JOURNALING:
CONSIDERING THE "SPIRITUAL BODY"

1. The Spiritual Body

So also is the resurrection from the dead. The body is sown in corruption, it is raised in incorruption. It is sown in dishonor, it is raised in glory. It is sown in weakness, it is raised in power. It is sown a natural body, it is raised a spiritual body. (I Corinthians 15: 42-44).

Journaling Question: *What is a **spiritual body**? Relax and let yourself imagine a spiritual "body image" for yourself. Describe it in some detail.*

As we have born the image of the man of dust, we shall also bear the image of the heavenly man.

"Burial of the Count of Orgaz"
(painting), El Greco, 1586

This well-known painting is very large, covering the whole wall of a small chapel in Toledo, Spain. (It can be enjoyed in color on the accompanying CD.) "The Burial of the Count of Orgaz" sets out a legendary intervention in which a good man is surrounded by loving friends, but is also being prepared for burial by St Francis and St. Augustine. The painter and his young son are also in the picture- suggesting a fluid sense of time. The elongated figures and vibrant colors are characteristic of El Greco's "mannerist" style. The painter came from Crete, a center of icon painting; it is easy to see this Eastern influence in his desire to spiritualize the body image. In this painting the fully mature artist has united the heavenly and earthly in a seamless vision. Perhaps the veil between us and the eternal world is thinner than we sometimes imagine it to be.

Here is an icon of Basil the Blessed, whose reputation and charisma were so powerful that even the autocrat Ivan the Terrible paid heed to his rebukes about social injustice. The image is a bas relief housed in the shrine of Basil within the colorful, multi-domed cathedral on Red Square in Moscow. Another icon, available on the CD, shows even more clearly the ascetic saint as a physical antithesis of the Greek ideal of beauty, the "fool for Christ" who nearly naked and haggard is able to see heavenly realities and speak transcendent wisdom. In this image depicting spiritualized human nature, we see some of what most Westerners notice in icons as unpleasant distortion, but what is meant

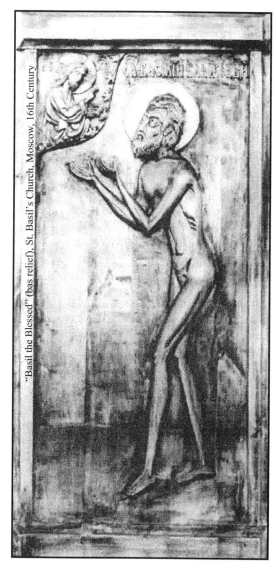

"Basil the Blessed" (bas relief), St. Basil's Church, Moscow, 16th Century

to be portrayed is the physical body purified, as it were, restored to Eden. Deeply furrowed brows, e.g., characterize spiritual wisdom. Body proportions usually conform to mathematical conventions that may seem distorted to eyes looking for literal realism. This style is meant to reveal the invisible, but fully real spiritual being, already manifest in certain holy persons this side of the grave. Aware of these conventional techniques and primed by the translation of these conventions by El Greco, can you, contemplating this image of "St. Basil the Blessed" or A. Rublev's "Blessed Basil and John of Moscow Contemplating the Holy Trinity," get in touch with spiritual reality squeezed into the physical dimension?

2. The Problem of Describing the Indescribable

The visual and verbal are neither the only, nor necessarily the best ways to communicate transcendent realities; music is another imaginative language and another way of evoking the mysterious beyond. Olivier Messiaen, for example, was a modernist composer with a strong mystical bent. He seemed to live firmly in this complex modern world, and yet to see beyond it. One of his masterpieces, *Quartet for the End of Time,* was written and first performed in a Nazi prison camp. A set of pipe organ pieces, *The Glorified Bodies: Seven Brief Visions of the Risen Life,* is meant to express the resurrection imagery of I Corinthians 15. The two selections you will hear on the CD are wonderfully successful in aurally communicating their titles: "The Joy and Clarity of the Glorified Bodies," and "The Force and Agility of the Glorified Bodies." The first piece evokes "the Just shining like the sun in their Father's kingdom;" the trumpet swirls and glints with explosive vitality like the improvisations of classic jazz. The second piece is a persistent, driving melody, unaccompanied until a few final dissonant chords crash on the ears, and then the sound dissipates like a vapor. Read again I Corinthians 15: 36–57 and then listen for yourself. **The trumpet will sound and the dead will be raised incorruptible, and we shall be changed** (I Cor. 15: 52).

(On the accompanying CD there is a recording of O. Messiaens's "Joie et Clarte des Corps Glorieux" and "Force et Agilite des Corps Glorieux"

from **Les Corps Glorieux**, performed by the author.)
Journaling Questions:

1.Have you ever had experiences beyond physical reality---something you would think of as "mystical?" If so, *how* would you communicate that to others? You have nothing to lose by taking on this task creatively.

"Light's abode, celestial Salem,
vision whence true peace doth spring,

Brighter than the heart can fancy,
mansion of the highest King.

O how glorious are the praises
which of thee the prophets sing!

O how glorious and resplendent,
fragile body, thou shalt be,

When endued with heavenly beauty,
full of health and strong and free.

Full of vigor, full of pleasure
that shall last eternally!"

What might this 15th Century hymn suggest to us today? Consider the mind-bending theories of current science and the many accounts of near-death experiences, what do you foresee 'out there.'" How do you expect to "be changed?"

LEGACY: REFLECTION AND JOURNALING

Thanks be to God who gives us the victory through our Lord Jesus Christ. Therefore, my beloved brethren, be steadfast, immovable,

always abounding in the work of the Lord, knowing that your labor is not in vain in the Lord (I Cor. 15: 57-58).

For Christians, the afterlife is assured. In the face of mortality, this passage indicates that there may be something that goes with us into the next life. Part of "abounding in the work of the Lord" involves awareness of our *legacy*: what we leave behind as we move on. There is much *moving on* over a lifetime, not just at physical death; consider final events like graduation from high school or college, changing jobs, divorce, leaving a professional sports career when past physical prime. These situations should cause us to ask, *"What is my legacy?"* This would be a useful question for journaling, sometimes planning follow-up action.

And in the light of eventual death we should have our legal Last Will in order; at whatever age we would have resources to leave behind, that reflect our values and the proper disposition of our possessions. Additionally, everyone should have a Living Will that gives instructions and designates a person who will do whatever needs to be done regarding the end of your life if you are unable to speak for yourself. Recently, another issue has created interest, the "Ethical Will." As we age, it becomes natural to embody the archetype of the Wise Elder. This means our advice is no longer seen as meddling and more likely to be considered "the wisdom of the tribe." (Ironically a respected woman in her late 80's, frequently speaks of her grandmother's abiding influence, and often quotes the spiritual wisdom she imparted long ago.)

Journaling: Here we suggest more than a journal entry. Consider writing the story of your life in stages. Concentrate on the situations and values ("guidelines for behavior") that formed your character. Make it a story, not just admonitions. If there were spiritual lessons that you learned or developed for yourself, be sure to include these as traditions that you would like to pass on -words of wisdom for your descendants. You could consider this project as a long letter written with family members in mind. Don't offer a list of precepts. Use a narrative style that describes how you came to this value and what it means.

WRITING YOUR OWN OBITUARY

It is said that one day Alfred Nobel, the inventor of dynamite, was reading the newspaper with his morning coffee when he came upon his obituary, mistakenly appearing in print. Mainly, he was to be remembered as the man who amassed a fortune by making the explosives used with devastating effect in World War I. This sobering article moved him to endow the famous prizes, the most important of which is the Nobel Peace Prize. Knowing the effect this obituary had on Mr. Nobel, maybe we can helpfully perform this exercise to begin moving through the awareness of our own mortality and into the blessing of living a life beyond death, even now. With this comes the chance to know the living God better for ourselves, and not just by hearsay.

Exercise in the imagination and journaling: *Before writing, relax and picture yourself at the wake before your own funeral. See yourself in the casket; notice who comes to pray and pay their respects to your family; listen to some of the conversations in your imagination. How is your family responding? Let this fantasy develop. If it gets uncomfortable, notice that feeling and try to see what lies behind it... Now pretend the casket is closed and begin to write your own obituary. Describe yourself in terms of your accomplishments and values (what you did about what you believed). Maybe come up with an interesting epitaph that you could imagine on your tombstone. Since this is only a fantasy, make some notes on what you would like to accomplish in the time you have left. Is there any unfinished personal business, or relationships that are not as you'd like to leave them, or anything important you have been putting off? What about God: are you ready to meet your Maker? Would you like to get to know God better on this side of eternity? This could be a very significant journal entry, so don't avoid it.*

SCRIPTURE REFLECTION: SIMEON & ANNA, THE WISE ELDERS

There are a few icons that tell a story in vignettes: the icon of the

Nativity is like that. It shows different parts of the story revolving around a dark cave with Mary and Jesus and the ox and ass at the center. The icon of the Presentation of Christ in the Temple is different. It does not tell Luke's story of the going up to Jerusalem, then the arrival and departure of the holy family. (Read the account and compare it to the image: Luke 2: 22 – 39). This icon is focused in on a single moment. Anna is not actively prophesying. Time has stopped, like a snapshot; and without denying the action, our attention is on "making present" –a principal theme of the Presentation story. Mary and Joseph behold the Christ, not just who Jesus is

"The Presentation of Christ in the Temple"

to them, but who Simeon, speaking by the Holy Spirit, says Jesus will be as the events of his unique life manifest the Messiah's life and work. This is a moment "in and out of time." Meditation on the event celebrated forty days after Christmas as Candlemas, where forever "all is calm, all is bright" can bring us into fuller awareness of what theologians have called "the real Presence of Christ." This is impossible to explain but is capable of being experienced spiritually. Like Simeon, we may become able to say, "Mine eyes have seen Thy salvation," and know a moment of God's eternal peace, like being on Heaven's front porch.

Look at Anna and Simeon. For us, they embody mature vision. That they are male and female seems fitting as signifying the whole of Israel. They recognize in their own experience, **that very hour,** the fulfillment of human life which we too may glimpse from time to time in moments of spiritual clarity, but which we will know in a sustained way only beyond death. Even the great saints like Paul had only sporadic glimpses of mature vision: **Now we see through a glass, darkly, but then face to face** (I Corinthians 13: 12). For those who seek "road signs" toward life's true destination, look no further. Surely, this is the substance of what Irenaeus meant: "The life of humanity is the vision of God."

Anna is a widow, eighty-four years old - an extreme age for the New Testament era. And yet her active life awaited its destiny. She has met the longed-for Messiah and will be the first to announce what she has seen. The prophetess becomes an evangelist. Any person up in years who wonders if there is still meaningful activity left to be done should remember Anna. Until our homecoming, there is always a reason to live.

Simeon's story is not revealed as a sequence of events (neither in Luke, nor in the icon), but there is an outline of it. He was *just, devout, waiting* for what God would provide, and *anointed* by the Holy Spirit to be in the right place at the right time, ready to truly see. (Luke 2: 25-32). These words could also be spoken of Anna. Perhaps if we develop these four characteristics, our capacity to know the "real Presence" and to represent Christ will increase.

The Eastern Church speaks of Simeon as the "Host of God." This icon reminds us there is a distinction but also a correspondence between recognizing the budding Messiah when his parents brought him to the Jerusalem Temple, and today's faithful receiving Christ, "veiled in Bread and Wine," as the priest places Him in our hands. Each Eucharist should be a unique temporal encounter with God. And yet each celebration is eternal. The aged Simeon and Anna represent both a culmination and a beginning. For centuries Israel has awaited God's promise of redemption, eventually expressed by hope for the Messiah. These *wise elders* are the climax of that hope. The infant Christ is placed in Simeon's welcoming arms, and his life is fulfilled, the future assured. At peace, he is ready to leave earthly life. It is sometimes said this old man is the first Christian (after Mary); the *host of God* he is called. The Feast of the Presentation comes forty days after Christmas on February 2. It is the mature culmination of Christmastide in a sense. God is truly with us, the ultimate desire fulfilled.

Journaling Questions: *How would I describe "just, devout, waiting and anointed?" What is the evidence of these four characteristics in my own life? How have I known Christ's Presence in Holy Communion? What actions have I taken as a result?*

THE HEART'S DEEPEST DESIRE

The following meditative sequence was prepared with Christmas in mind, but it embodies the all-seasonal quest for spiritual maturity which the wise elders, Simeon and Anna represent. It can be experienced profitably any time of the year. The script should be read to a group; it takes about thirty minutes including six minutes to hear *Nimrod*, from Sir Edward Elgar's "Enigma Variations." The leader may choose to use introductory sections 1 or 2 separately; 1 is specifically focused on Christmastide; 2 is more general. Groups as well as individuals may prefer the version recorded on the accompanying CD. But the leader may also prefer to read the script below and play an orchestral version of *Nimrod*:

1. Layers of Desire (5 minutes)

Children everywhere are waiting for Christmas…There is an atmosphere of excitement, anticipation. Parents and grand parents have asked "What do you want?" …What would make you happy under the Christmas tree? There will be new toys; some becoming old quickly, some becoming favorites… The child in each of us has shifting desires. And desires change with age. What would you like, if you could have anything at all, as your heart's desire for Christmas? Imagine a wrapped box, a present…visualize it and unwrap. "Surprise, what's inside?" (Pause 30 sec.)

Desires may range from accessible to impossible, good for us or maybe a curse. We know we cannot, should not have everything we want. We can't all be movie stars. Mansions have to be cleaned and taxes paid. Still everyone wants the better things, for self and for others. Desires are complex with deep roots.

Seeking the meaning of what we want, reveals deeper layers of desire, like peeling away an onion. For example: (As a ten year old, shortly after my father's death I prayed for a bicycle for Christmas. I declined to tell my mother, who surely could not afford such an extravagance. When the gift didn't materialize, I projected the anger about my father's death, and resented other more fortunate children; I felt isolated and abandoned and I felt guilty about my desire since I knew my mom was struggling to provide for us. I stopped praying for a long time. Only as an adult did I remember the bicycle I had a few months later- still don't remember where it came from. That deeply desired bike was both a symbol of grief and a promise of freedom [*This illustration may be replaced with the leader's own*]). Desires are not often simple or pure. For Christians there is a sobriety about human nature. It is precisely the level of desire that gets us into so much trouble. There is forbidden fruit, and each of us has tasted. As St. Paul said, "All have sinned, and fall short of the glory of God."

Beyond this or even within it, is the ultimate desire. The longing for God is universal."O come, Emmanuel… O come, desire of nations." Christians long for a cleansing of desire, a healing that will conform us to our ultimate happiness. We hope to share God's desire. We await the day of His coming. Not just in December, Christian spirituality embraces a perpetual Advent. Our faith is "the assurance of things hoped for, the conviction of things not seen." We always cultivate the awareness, however dim, that the King has come, is coming, will come in glory. No Christmas gift could ever be enough. It is Christ himself we long for. Any year if we can glimpse the light that shines in darkness, it will suffice.

In the fall of the third grade, I first experienced the longing for a real Christmas. I remember thinking several times: *Less than four months to go.* Surprisingly, presents and Santa weren't part of the fantasy. It was something else. I remember pressing my face to the window at night, feeling the coolness, looking for something ineffable, for something beyond. There was music on the radio that made me teary. What was my heart's desire? What was to come?

In a way, life as a Christian could be described simply as three intertwined movements of desire: Experiencing the purification of our desires in an atmosphere of grace; Learning to find God's desire for us; Acting in conformity with God's desire to the extent we are aware and able.

2. The Way of Unknowing (10 minutes)

Just now I invite you to enjoy a meditative time focused on desire, actually the healing of desire. First we will consider a couple of things:

A. The first consideration: I want to show you a way to "put the mind in the heart," as the Orthodox put it. This is metaphorical, of course; but let us not say it is *merely a* metaphor. There is a place in conscious awareness that is deeper than ordinary thinking. Once you have located it, with a little practice you will know when you have entered the "heart." Awareness of our desires is usually obscured by memories and routines of thought; and this awareness is filtered through self-censorship. Still the deeper place of desire can be entered directly. It is not the same as asking "What do I want?" This is too mental. It involves longing for what you want intuitively. For many it is just below the level of tears. In the meditation time, you may be moved inside or want to weep. If this happens take a deep breath and go deeper, relax and find what I call *the place of desires*. There are several ways to do this, but I have found that listening to a certain kind of music opens the heart and leads to unfocused, pure desire. Classical music of the Romantic Period is often structured to have this effect. There could be a multitude of choices, something you might experiment with. Today we will listen to the *Nimrod* movement from Sir Edward Elgar's "Enigma Variations". It is a passionately romantic piece that builds on wave after wave of rising emotion to a moment of intense desire and then subsides peacefully. It does not evoke desire for anything in particular, just a longing so intense it seems to bring one into another state of consciousness. I want you to experience this "naked desire" and sustain it if possible in a period of prayer.

B. Now the second thing to consider: In order to turn this into a prayer of longing for God, we will use the classic method from the little English medieval manual, <u>The Cloud of Unknowing</u>. The basic premise of this writer, as with all teachers of mystical prayer, is that God cannot be directly known in this life, except by love. This is why one should come at it with the heart open from a place of naked desire. This longing love will be directed only to God. The author speaks of two inner images, the Cloud of Forgetting, and above it, the Cloud of Unknowing. Thoughts or images of any kind should be released as soon as they come to awareness into the Cloud of Forgetting. The person praying remains with naked desire, directed toward the Cloud of Unknowing where God abides and from whence many blessings will come. (Those of you who practice centering prayer will find this similar.) It is the element of the *Heart's Desire* that is emphasized: "Beat on the Cloud with arrows of love," the author says. Beware the imagery. This all takes place beyond imagination. It is not like imagining a blank movie screen, or a puffy cloud, or a Valentine's Cupid.

Guided meditation period. (15 minutes)

(The audio script on the CD begins here, if the leader wants to use

it after reading section 1 or 2.)

"Now I invite you to experience the deepest desire of your heart through music, and then to turn this longing into prayer awaiting God's blessing:"

Start the *Nimrod* movement (approximately 6 minutes) with instruction for quiet relaxation: feet to head; tense and relax, especially the neck and shoulders.

Now think of something you desire, or sort through some desires. Imagine this with senses... **Pause about 60 seconds.**

Now let go all objects and concerns. Listen to the music and let the phrases lead you to the place of naked desire and rest there. If you become emotional, take a breath and relax with the swelling music...

In a few minutes of silence, let thoughts go. Direct your heart's longing in faith and hope to God.

At the end of fifteen minutes or so, close the meditation period slowly and deliberately:

O come Emmanuel,
Key of David,

O come Prince of Peace,
Desire of Nations
Bind in one the hearts of all mankind.
Bid Thou our sad divisions cease;
And be Thyself our King of Peace

So Jacob was left alone, and a man wrestled with him there till daybreak. When the man saw he could not throw Jacob, he struck him in the hollow of his thigh, so that Jacob's hip was dislocated as they wrestled. The man said, "Let me go for day is breaking," but Jacob replied, "I will not let you go unless you bless me."

He said to Jacob, "What is your name?"

"Your name shall no longer be Jacob, but Israel, because you strive with God and with men and prevailed!"

Gen 32

CHAPTER NINE

DREAMS
&
THE SPIRITUAL ARCHETYPES

Together with prayer and Bible study, working with dreams is a traditional and potent tool for enriching spiritual development. Of course, we dream several times each night and tend to remember those just before waking in the morning, if only for a brief period. Most dreams seem to be a way to cleanse the mind of emotional debris, often balancing the slate. One can for example, have a familiar anxiety dream and wake completely refreshed. This dream has served its function, and we forget about it. But there are dreams that arise from time to time from the deeper places in the personal unconscious. These can bring creative ideas, solutions to troubling problems, warnings and other useful things. The collective unconscious, that deep well of cultural and racial memory, also reveals itself in dreams, especially if we begin to pay attention to what is often called, "the dark speech of dreams." The archetypes in the various phases we have touched on also appear in dreams, and can respond to the kind of journal reflection we have been practicing.

Some dreams can be filled with spiritual insight and power. In scripture, the dream has been viewed suspiciously; by Jeremiah, for example, who made a clear distinction between dreams and the prophetic word. But some extremely important revelations have come through dreams. There was Jacob's wonderful covenant revelation, delivered in the dream of a ladder to heaven on which angels (messengers) went back and forth to bless him. The annunciation of Jesus to Joseph was in a dream, as was the warning to take the child and his mother, and flee to Egypt from Herod's wrath. There are several other significant dreams recorded in scripture. And God still frequently reveals himself the same way - to bring wisdom, encouragement and guidance to those who are prayerfully attentive to their dreams. During the first thousand years of church history, dream-work was at the heart of spiritual exploration. It was expected that God would personally reveal himself in dreams just as he had in scripture, as Pilate's wife, for example, told her husband she had dreamed he should "have nothing to do with this innocent man." Also, at deep levels, meditation tends to encourage visions that are dreamlike in character. And then there are charismatic spiritual gifts that can come forth as easily sleeping as in the waking state. We should be open to spiritual experience and pay attention to dreams. The literature is vast. A number of books in categories such as physiology, psychology and spirituality of dreams to which this summation is indebted would be useful resources for further exploration.[16]

Actually, like regular personal prayer, dream work is within the ability of everyone, but too often neglected. With a little practice of daily attention to dreams, we will meet important parts of our deeper self and become open to spiritual revelations. If you are working with a small group a period of sharing dreams can be helpful by bringing this material out into the daylight. Some groups gather just for dream work for a period of time. The method below was tested in such a setting. In our experience, listening to the dreams of others can be nearly as insightful as working with your own.

Here is a basic way to use dreams as part of the spiritual journey:

A DREAM-WORK MODEL

Preparation and Expectations. Provide yourself with a special notebook to use as a dream journal. Keep it next to your bed and prepare to make short entries, usually no more than a page. Leave room for later journal style reflection on this material. Be prepared to note down the dream on waking without other activity. Even a short sentence or a couple of strong images may be enough to keep the dream from leaving your waking awareness. A snippet remembered is likely to be the part you need to recall. Not all dreams are worth consideration; but you may be surprised at dream images and memories coming to mind later in the day, just

---

[16]Morton T Kelsey, God, Dreams and Revelation (Augsburg, 1991) is suggested. For many others, note the Bibliography.

because you jot something down. There are several dream cycles during the night. (These periods are well documented by dream researchers because of the rapid eye movement that occurs - REM episodes.) Occasionally you will awaken in the night with a powerful dream that you can write about and then return to sleep. Most remembered dreams take place just on the edge of waking and sleeping. In your journal, enter the date and approximate time of the dream; if there was something significant about the day, (birthday, lost your job, etc.), mention that too. The surrounding context is generally important. Also, note how you, not the "dreamer," felt on waking. Words are not the only or best way to record a dream; sketching, using colors, or even doodles may be expressive and meaningful on examination.

The Basic Journal Entry. Jot down the actual dream story without explanatory comment or analysis. A few sentences will suffice, like a sketch of essentials instead of a whole landscape. Often there will be a series of stories that seem unrelated. Or, your scenario may have a straight-forward beginning, middle and end. Sometimes, often perhaps, the story is unfinished. Take what comes; and gently honor whatever you remember. Even a single image with no story can be significant. The goal should not be to take a stenographic record of night-time brain activity from the inner point of view! (That is a recipe for wakefulness and data overload.) Take what lingers on the edge of sleep as it comes, and don't become overly involved with thinking about it.

Attitude. The way you approach dream work is important. Certainly, if your unconscious mind wants to get a message across, you will remember it. Even then, much inner communication is lost because our world tends to devalue this material with such ideas as: "You must be dreaming!" "Did you have garlic for dinner?" Or, that childhood antidote to nightmares: "It was just a dream. Go back to sleep." Good dream-work is like entertaining unknown but invited guests. Be hospitable. Dreams, even recurring ones, will often have subtle elements of surprise. An analytical attitude, or even great curiosity, may crush a dream's capacity to manifest and maybe expand its presence. Dream-work is like watching a butterfly move from flower to flower. One may enjoy it, relate to it in some way, observing different things. To catch the butterfly and dissect it is another process with an entirely different outcome. Consider the dream to be living; don't kill it. One of the reasons to "befriend" dreams – Carl Jung's word, is that they come with blessings. Even scary and sinister dreams have positive value when we welcome them. To become fully conscious, we must permit dreams to come to us. This seems an odd requirement in face of the fact that the dream world, like sleeping, exists whether or not we deprive ourselves of it and ignore or discount it. Dreams should be allowed to reveal their secrets. We will strive in vain to fasten interpretations on them. And we should not pay attention when others dogmatize about meanings. Our dreams will disclose themselves, meanings and all, if we really listen to them, especially for what is still unknown. The essential attitude is listening with the heart. Easy to say, this takes practice.

Reflection. This means write another paragraph or so about the script sometime later in the day. Clearly mark this return to the dream as a reflection, also note the time. The TTAQ outline, recommended in the book <u>Dreams and Spiritual Growth</u>[17] may serve well as a starter for reflection, though some will struggle with so much structure. The outline is:

A. Give the dream a TITLE,

B. Then in a sentence or two, express what seems to be its THEME.

C. Ask yourself what feelings are evoked and expressed in the dream itself: This is the AFFECT.

D. Then, instead of asking the obvious, "What does this mean?" Let the dream QUESTION you, "What does it ask of me?"

Some further suggestions: The title will come without assistance; write down the first thing that comes to mind. The theme is usually your expansion of the title, what the dream seems to be about. Every dream, if nothing else, portrays feelings, often with different characters. Sometimes there is a series or development or resolution of feelings. Usually the basic emotional tone of the dream is not what you feel on waking. A single word probably won't say enough. For example, not "He was sad;" but, "He was

---

[17]L. Savary, P. Berne & K. Williams, <u>Dreams and Spiritual Growth, A Christian Approach to Dreamwork</u> (Paulist Press, 1988)

sad like watching the tide gradually wash away a sandcastle." This further description should seem real at the time, not fantastic but part of the dream's self-disclosure. A typical dream-inspired question might be: "Is it really necessary for me to be so angry today?" Or, "Maybe I should do something down to earth?" after a flying dream, etc. The questions also come intuitively.

A SAMPLE JOURNAL ENTRY

Significant dreams can be of many types. The following is an account of a search for help seeking a dreamed solution. One may recall, the ancients practiced *incubation*, for example, sleeping in a temple of Aesculapius in hopes of a curative dream. You too may want to "sleep on" a personal concern. (Dreamers have often reported solutions to major problems and creative insights- some famously publicized.) Healing may also be part of the process as in my case – freely then, using the TTAQ model:

Title and Theme: Blessed Change: An inner healing
The Context: date, time, location (if relevant). "After an insult I became more upset than I could remember. I felt angry and vengeful, but not violent. After some name-calling I withdrew, but continued to tremble for several minutes. Beneath the anger I felt wounded. I went to bed with the intention of offering it all to God, including the inability to get past it or to forgive. For what seemed like hours of semi-consciousness I *observed* vindictive thoughts and explanations of the situation –refused to get involved, let the thoughts fizzle out. Then came the pivotal core dream. As the night wore on I continued to have the unsettling thoughts, but that state of mind diminished with each of several periods of dreaming. The dreams, in which I was always aware of myself dreaming, grew more complex each time. It felt like I was being reconfigured from the inside, like rebooting perhaps – not uncomfortable, but I was aware I would not recall the expansive stories of these colorful dreams. When morning came and I

awoke, it seemed like I had slept little; but I was completely refreshed. The incident of the night before was firmly behind me; the poisonous aftermath of the incident was gone, like mist in the sunlight. I had experienced an inner healing that left me feeling joyful, thankful that the incident had happened, and energized in anticipation of the new day."

The Dream Story: The simple, brief incident had a very clear atmosphere, a sunny day: *I was on the tarmac walking alone to board a small plane. A man was in the path selling newspapers. He was dark, Hispanic I thought. I handed him a $20 bill for a paper; but he couldn't make change. He spoke only Spanish and did not understand my concern about change. I was hesitant, but didn't refuse when he handed me a large envelope with the paper. Opening it I was surprised to find the exact change, but also a quantity of fine cheese with a pack of crackers, a perfect snack for the plane trip*

Reflection: Upon waking, I shared the dream story with my wife who knew about the last evening's incident. She noticed the problem with "making change," and saw it as about making personal changes. Surprisingly, I hadn't noticed this double meaning. She also noted the dark guy may be a shadow figure. This also seemed right to me; an *A-ha!* of recognition came with both suggestions.

On reflection (in my journal), this whole incident with the dream at its core, seemed to me a serendipitous moment that depicted the healing that was taking place –a metaphor for an otherwise invisible personal restoration. I recalled having heard in the night the Psalm verse: **He gives his beloved sleep**. I was willing to be willing to change, and was blessed with actual change –plus a gratuitous surprise snack, the joyous feeling of restoration that remained for the journey.

+++++++++

If one is writing about a dream that seems to be momentous or revelatory, two techniques used by psychoanalysts may be used for the written reflection: **Amplification**- this is to allow yourself to develop other instances of this or similar images. Jungians delight in making mythic, folkloric and religious connections; the more arcane the better. The other technique is **Association.** This means to gently allow your mind to make connections with other memories. Often the intuitive function makes surprising but significant connections. One should be warned about too much analytical intellectualizing in dream-work. The process is largely emotional, intuitive and symbolic- each dimension having its own ways of making sense. Often a dream revelation creates a physical tingling sensation, or some inner voice wants to say, "A-ha!" The truth value of this kind of reflection seems to be self-authenticating. This is why other persons' dream interpretations and popular books explaining dream symbolism are not usually helpful.

The deeper levels of awareness will seek to disclose themselves to us, but usually this will be in the form of stories and symbols. This is after all, the native language of dreams, which will interpret themselves if we give heed. Often interpretation is not the purpose of dream work; one may never understand exactly what a certain dream means, even years later; but there will always emerge a broader awareness, and often creativity is enhanced; and energy to improve something will start to flow from the process. Journaling is indeed a powerful tool for this.

Jung himself took a *phenomenological* approach to dreams, observing without judgment what occurs, and like a good scientist, giving the inner data room to be and perhaps speak to us. (More contemporary dream researchers have a very wide range of understanding about dreams and what to do with them.)

THE ARCHETYPES AS THEY OCCUR IN DREAMS

There are several archetypes that frequent dreams when they emerge from the unconscious depths; their forms are diverse, but types are limited. Here are some helps from a Jungian perspective to recognize the basic symbols which may portray themselves in unique ways:

Animus/Anima. A character of the opposite sex often appears in dreams, which Jung said represented the psyche or soul, female for men, male for women. This character helps to shed light upon many relational attractions when we analyze the psychological phenomenon of *projection*. The idea of finding one's "soul-mate" relates to this, creating potential for a love relationship that transcends ordinary friendship among trusted companions. Jung also thought that the modern world was suffering from a vast loss of soul, which could account for some of our culture's alienation, and the absorption in and identification with life's glittering surface, while engaging in mind-numbing pastimes and addictions. For us, it may be just as important to reclaim the soul's life, as it is to develop the spirit. Befriending dreams will eventually bring one to encounter the soul as a complete young man or woman. Jung had an encounter over many years with such a character.

Many famous mystics entered into dialogue with the soul, most notably Catherine of Siena and John of the Cross. Some have practiced journaling as a dialogue between *self* (perhaps the person aware of dreaming) and *soul*. If you attempt this, let the *animus-anima* speak for itself. Be prepared to listen and record. Then participate in the dialogue as your *conscious* self.

JOURNALING EXERCISE: THE GARDEN

Another image of the soul is symbolized by gardens. The Bible begins and ends in a paradisal garden. The first Adam's job was to tend and manage God's creation, and then to till the soil. The second Adam was interred in the new tomb of Joseph of Aramathea in a garden near Golgotha. Three days later, Mary Magdalene at first mistook Jesus for the gardener. All these images are evocative of something in the soul. Play some quiet music, and then:

Relax and remember some gardens you have read about or known personally. Get a feeling for each one and consider what is memorable about them...Now enter the garden of your soul. It can have any size or shape and be like anything you wish. After this image settles in the mind, enter and explore it with all your senses...You see someone up ahead; it is

Jesus. Go to him and speak of your garden, the soul, and listen to what he has to say...When you are ready, leave the garden as you entered it. You will return from time to time.

(There is an audio version of this meditation on the CD.)

The Persona. This is the socialized part of the self. In dreams this character has individual awareness and feelings and several frequently recurring roles, like one's job or place in the family or other group. One could say: "In my dream I saw myself doing..." In this statement there are two "*I*-s" –the first is the *ego* speaking from the waking state, the other, clearly separate, is "myself," the *persona*. When I put my best foot forward, conforming to what is required and expected by myself and others; I create a mask, or several. I might be one person at work and another in various relationships: employee, husband, wife, child, mother, father, or other family role. These masks (often called *personas*) represent "not what one is, but what oneself, as well as others, think one is."[18] The inner person, self-aware (usually called the *ego*) wears and controls these various masks without recognizing that he is doing this. Sometimes the *ego* loses track of who he is and the masks "live him." The famous Italian movie actor Marcello Mastroiani was quoted in an interview: "Life is just a game in which I pretend to love." Self-awareness requires looking under the masks, and intimacy involves sharing the inner self with others, or there will be a painful crisis of identity. Much of modern life requires pretense; so much so that the journey inward requires one to look at the unknown within; this may call one to face the fear that what is inside is unacceptable or worthless. Those who have taken the risk of journeying deeper have universally affirmed the value of the work and the beauty of their ultimate discoveries.

Over the years, I have had a series of dreams involving my work life. I think of these as anxiety dreams because they embody fear. I have noticed that the *me* in these dreams is tense and fidgety; but the waking self, sometimes aware of the dream while dreaming it, is refreshed, peaceful, and ready to move along with the day. If we pay attention to such common

---

[18] Carl Jung, <u>Collected Works, IX</u>, I, paragraph 221.

dreams over time, the images change and we develop a healthier relationship with various life "roles." Such dream-work will eventually bring integration of outer and inner parts of the self.

Here is another example of a significant *persona* dream. It has never faded into memory and occurred some time prior to any journaling with dreams. I still remember the dream clearly. (Its brightness and transparency, like peering through a window, seem to indicate little work needed to be done either to accept or to understand the dream.) Shortly after our newborn first child came home from the hospital, I awoke and shared this dream with my wife:

I saw myself in a large entry porch of an imaginary home. Inside were painters and carpenters building an additional room, a nursery. I knew my wife and baby daughter were in there some place, but with all the construction work, I couldn't get their attention. I knocked at the door and tapped on the windows. I felt lonely and isolated, locked out of the place where I belonged.

The man on the porch, *persona* as lover, husband and father, was vaguely visible, partly separate from the dreaming self, also present but distinct and invisible. When I woke and shared this dream with my wife we both chuckled and instantly understood what was going on. The dream embodied my feelings about this new situation. I got up, took the baby from her bassinet, gave her to my wife for a little refreshment and tears began to flow. This seems to be the exact moment I became a *parent*. And the dream was naturally part of the transformational process. During the last few hectic days, working and going back and forth to the maternity ward, I didn't have much feeling about the baby or the whole event. I had looked forward for months to sharing this whole thing with my wife. I had spoken of this odd disappointment with an older friend who said "not to worry." He hadn't felt much connection with his children until they were old enough to play with him. I remembered this related incident after the dream while making breakfast, and knew that somehow my friend had given me permission to accept the way I felt; these were the feelings I blocked out of awareness by judging them inappropriate to what I wanted to feel.

This dream script was never actually written until now. Together with my reflections, it is provided as another example of dream-work and its place in life. Most journaling with dreams is less clear or one would never forget them, as above; but this activity begins a process with its own creative life. Consider writing some journal reflections with the intent to explore and reveal your inner *persona*. This work can have surprising emotional and spiritual value.

Journaling Exercise: *Other than journaling with words, one should also be encouraged to use other means of expression. Some part of the persona archetype will be a good place to begin. Create with paints, clay or some other medium, an image of yourself as you think you are or want to be seen. The representation need not be accurate or even skillfully produced. For this exercise you should allow your unconscious to shape the work. Proportions, colors, distortions or other details will be significantly displayed by what you have produced. This may be an image that appeared in a dream that you will amplify artistically or it may be an image that emerges in the waking state with your permission. Relax into the creative process. Allow your persona to do a self-portrait. One does not need to have much artistic talent or skill to do this; though for artists such activity is part of the tricks of the trade. Everyone should have the experience of artistic expression. It is a corrective to the spectator mentality and consequent passivity of current culture. Such projects, by stimulating the deeper self, will be healthful both psychologically and spiritually. You may want to reflect in your journal on what you have made. Gaze upon the object quietly. What does it say to you…about itself…about you?*

The Shadow. This part of the personality is often hard to locate. The shadow is the "ground" upon which the conscience rests. It is the first element of the deep self to enter awareness. This image contains all the things we would like to hide, or defensively to project onto others. The shadow will eventually reveal itself, but we can assist the process and begin to distinguish it from the conscious self by using two techniques:

Consider the masks just described and list all the positive qualities you find, e.g., "rugged strength". Then list the opposite of these things. This activity may offer a general structure of the shadow personality repressed just below the civilized surface.

List the people and kinds of persons you don't like or who make you feel uncomfortable. Especially notice the people you feel an emotional need or desire to criticize or judge. If you have any enemies, note them. Then consider what it is that bothers you in each case.

These two exercises will seem artificial, but it may be that by "priming the pump" your inner shadow will become clearer to you soon. When this happens, be willing to accept an inner stranger.

The shadow character has been frequently portrayed in literature and film. Perhaps the most famous scenario is "Peter Pan," where the central character has lost his shadow, and thus cannot, or will not mature. As the story develops, he grows up with the help of an inner fairy woman (Tinkerbell), and an outer friend who loves him (Wendy), and who can sew on shadows for lost boys. Captain Hook, of course, is the perfect image of amoral, self-centered childishness and is also a shadow characterization. (One of the movie versions managed to have Peter and Hook played by the same actor.) This story is symbolically resonant, and like so many other mythic and "fairy tale" plots, has been used therapeutically as well as for entertainment. Such classic stories as "Dr. Jekyll and Mr. Hyde," "Frankenstein" and "The Portrait of Dorian Gray," resonate by touching psychological characters in everyone's unconscious mind. But, sometimes it seems, we receive so much external input from entertainments that we neglect doing the inner work of becoming a *fully human person* by exploring and integrating- and even redeeming, our own personal manifestations of the universal archetypes.

Many persons have had dreams of flight from a frightening, pursuing presence. The one chasing is the **shadow.** In the process of this recurring dream, the fleeing person may eventually turn and face the pursuer, to find this is to meet one's twin, or perhaps to meet oneself as for the first time. When these images occur in dreams, they may seem less interesting than the classic entertainment or crime shows on TV, but they are real and are calling for attention. Shadow dreams always have a sinister and fearful atmosphere, so we tend to ignore them if possible, like children's "bad dreams." But on giving permission through journaling, good things can begin to happen inside. From these images and reflections, wisdom will pass unobstructed into daytime life. By recognizing what a certain image means to you - this requires "befriending" the image - its terrors diminish and the energy becomes positive and creative. The explorer will expand the boundaries of awareness and discover new energy and insights into ongoing issues. You may begin experiencing this rich inner personality, truly a part of oneself, by paying attention to dark or invisible characters in dreams. Even the shaded, or colorless (or whatever) atmosphere of many dreams deserves exploration. There will be surprises, and the inner depths are literally unfathomable. But be encouraged, not afraid to proceed.

The Wise Elders. Characters from different stages of the life cycle are all spiritually significant when they appear in dreams, as one will have gathered from the presentation and explorations of the several *phases* in this book. Children, adults, even infant characters usually have a multi-layered meaning in dreams which will best be explored through journaling about them. Remember that dream characters, especially those representing familiar persons, are not those persons but manifestations of one's own psyche. (It is possible for deep spiritual contact from distinctly *other* beings to be made in dreams; but this is rare and should be considered unusual – and with some care.) The mature person in dreams is a frequent and most helpful visitor. Often the wise elder takes the shape of trusted grandparent (who in fact naturally embodies this part of the archetype). If, say, an old grade school teacher or dear grandmother appears in a dream, pay attention, and do extra journaling reflection. These characters always bring some practical word of wisdom you need to assimilate and usually to apply in current situations.

Animals. Many kinds of creatures occur in dreams. Some talk. Some are familiar pets. There are composite animals. Totem animals emerge; media images from cartoons may visit your dreams. The possibilities are infinite. Let us say in general, these characters usually have a spiritual value. In more nature-grounded cultures than ours, animal imagery has

---

always had practical spiritual significance. Since the collective unconscious is universal and timeless, images may emerge from many sources. Children will easily describe the animals they know, not just pets and stuffed toys, but lions and totem figures that visit their dreams to bring a sense of power to those who often feel small and helpless. Listening to other cultures may once again open us to a renewed encounter with the sacred depths of nature. If there are animals or other creatures in your dreams, even aliens, don't hesitate to get to know them and listen to what personal messages they bring. Even if they don't talk, with a bit of reflection meanings will come forth.

Angels and Demons. Such presences are actually quite common and may appear in different forms. They obviously carry spiritual messages and influences that one should recognize and then respond carefully.

Over the years I have found that when people are warmly invited to share their deeper experience without criticism, frequently spiritual presences will be discussed. Some years ago a woman in a dream workshop brought her friend who came because she thought others, especially in her church, would laugh at something very important to her. She had been faithful to her religious up-bringing over many years, but none of it seemed very real to her. Something, she always knew, was missing. One night she awoke, (Was she literally dreaming the awake state - who can say? Does it matter?) There was a "being" (her word) clothed in a brown robe seated at the foot of her bed. Without fear, she gazed at this being for some time, and when it left, she said her religious sense had changed. What had seemed a matter of pious habit now seemed vibrant and meaningful. This woman was surprised and reassured to hear other members of the group relate angelic encounters and what they meant to them... Recall from scripture that angels are messengers and what they communicate tends to have great energy and value.

Of course, demonic beings also may come to us. Eastern Orthodox monks have always described periods of demonic attack and spiritual battle, which tend to diminish as spiritual life matures. And there was Martin Luther for whom the demonic seemed so- was so concrete, he once threw his inkwell at the Devil. When this sort of thing happens to Christians, waking or in dreams, nothing is necessary for us except to turn our attention to God. Take the name of Jesus, and evoke his eternal person. St. Paul was probably quoting an early Christian hymn, from a culture attuned to a wide range of spiritual realities, when he wrote: **At the name of Jesus every knee should bow, in heaven and on earth and under the earth, and every tongue confess that Jesus Christ is Lord, to the glory of God the Father.** (Philippians 2:10-11). In general, to pay much attention to the demonic is unwise. In deep prayer such experiences occur from time to time. The wisdom of the ages has taught us to ignore such things and they will dissipate. Spiritual attention should be focused on God alone.

++++++++++

There is a meditation on the accompanying CD, "Six Moments with Christ," that explores the several phases of the Hero archetype as they are related to the scriptural life of Jesus. It may be useful as an exercise for journaling at this point.

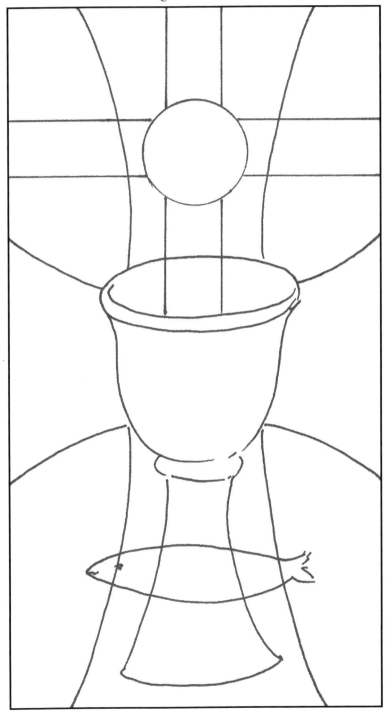

CHAPTER TEN

SIX MOMENTS WITH CHRIST
EXPLORING THE ARCHETYPE OF JESUS THE HERO

Read this script in sync with an orchestral recording of "Appalachian Spring" by Aaron Copland.

Follow the recording as directed in the script; or, use the enclosed CD (The organ background is "Adagietto" from "Symphony Number Four" by Gustave Mahler) when exploring alone.

The silences are timed to the musical shifts. After the Ignatian style guided meditation participants will reflect in their journals. Then a group sharing period will follow. The session requires about 55 minutes.

+++++++++

This is a safe place, and a time designed to experience something of the richness of God's love for us, even God's gracious presence... Take a minute to become relaxed and quiet. Just close your eyes; then release the tension in your body and get comfortable... First of all, become aware of your breathing; breathe slowly and very deeply so that your body is cleansed and saturated with oxygen. We will need to be alert, not sleepy... [*Start music. Wait 20 seconds; and then begin.*] As you listen to the music, notice the rhythm of your breathing. If there is anything you've been concerned about, let that go as you breathe out... Now let your imagination turn to a scene you find restful. Allow it to take shape in your mind's eye. Let the calm of this experience spread throughout your body like a gentle rain soaking into thirsty ground. Let there be a sense of peace, quiet, energy and focus... "The Lord is my shepherd, therefore I lack nothing."

[*Offer this invocation, 2 minutes into the recording.*] **Lord, send us your Holy Spirit, so that as we rest our bodies in your Presence, and our minds in calming thought, we may also rest our spirits in your life-giving truth; and may better come to know the Christ who is within,**

the hope of glory. Amen.

Now we will experience several moments in the life of Jesus as recorded in the Bible. These scenes were six events in his earthly life. But they are also eternal moments, where God is able to touch us as contemporaries. Remember, Jesus who once was, and is now with us, just as he promised. The eyes of faithful imagination can open a grace-filled encounter with the One who is the same today, yesterday and tomorrow.

1. [*Wait until 3:05 minutes; the music changes dramatically.*] In the first scene I want to call to mind, Jesus is about two years old. Let it take shape in your imagination. He can surely walk and talk, but as toddlers do. Allow yourself to experience the Christ child still living in Bethlehem. It is late afternoon of the day when Joseph's dream directed him to flee to Egypt for the child's protection. And so, imagine Jesus with his family: Joseph and Mary in a small house on a narrow street in Bethlehem. It is no longer the Inn, but another temporary place. Look at Jesus walking around on small feet, a toddler not too sure of his footing, but confidant he can walk anywhere he wants. He aims for Mary and climbs up into her lap. It's getting toward evening. He snuggles down as Joseph begins to tell a story. We can't hear the words; but Jesus can. They comfort him and calm him for the night's rest. [*Pause until 4:28 minutes*] Looking in the window is a stranger from far, far away – surely one of the Magi. Moonlight touches the expectant wise man, slants through the window, and bathes the child with an oval of moon-glow. It is the dawn of his remembering- a moment of cozy warmth, reverent with mystery. In your mind's eye enter this scene for a few moments. Where are you in the picture? How do you feel?

2. [*Pause until 5:40, when the music changes again.*] Now we turn to a second scene in the life of Jesus as he grows. It's getting on toward dusk. He is on the great staircase of the temple, sitting with legs stretched out, twelve years old, maturing. The strapping lad has been talking with the rabbis in the Temple court. He left just as some of these elders, clearly impressed with his potential, tried to engage him in yet another test case in the Law. Looking around at the great city from the Temple Mount he suddenly feels quite lonely, and realizes his parents are no longer around.

Alone and feeling abandoned, he doesn't have enough experience to know what to do next. He decides to wait - wait to be found. Calmly he turns within and finds his ABBA, the One whose business he must be about. He rests there. He may be lost on the outside; but turning inside he is always at home... Take a place in this scene with Jesus the boy. Can you feel the energy radiating from his presence?

3. [*Pause until 7:15 minutes, then:*] Now let's move toward a third scene. Jesus is very much a man now, robust from working in construction with Joseph and the other men of Nazareth, he is ready to move on to his own mission, however it might unfold. He has gone to his cousin John, and been baptized by him in the Jordan. The Father is well-pleased. Now join Jesus in this picture. He is in the Judean wilderness. The time is midday and quite warm. You see him walking, sandals stirring the dust. The sun bears down. There have been no marked paths as he moves through the desert. Searching for the right way to fulfill the call to action is also strenuous. There can be no short-cuts or compromises. Sometimes his mind has swarmed with chaos and illusions, but no more. He stands against alternatives that are not right for him. He returns, leaving the Tempter, to struggle another day... Walk along with him. Notice the warm dust in your sandals. Smell the desert breeze... How does it feel to walk with Jesus?... Do you have choices to make? Draw your strength from him.

4. [*Pause until 9:38 minutes*] Now we will enter a fourth scene. There has been constant activity –much teaching, many healings. A large crowd gathers and friends follow along... Into this scene a gentile woman comes up from behind. Jesus is moving towards a place where he will say things never to be forgotten. But then she interrupts - touches the hem of his garment. He feels energy draining from him. In the split second before he turns to respond, Jesus is annoyed. He is getting very tired. He thinks of the many days he has spent walking, teaching, and healing. How difficult it has been to be so available, to put his own needs to one side so others' can be met. Later there will be time for refreshment. He gathers his strength and once again turns to speak and bless. Watch him for a minute as he gives new life... Where are you in this scene? Is there a word, or healing touch,

just for you?

5. [*Pause until 12:15 minutes.*] Consider one more scene, and then one last one. This moment late in Jesus' earthly life is a time to engage in focused conflict. He stands before the tomb of his friend who has now been dead four days. He is flanked by mourners and realists, yet he will say what we know he said, "Lazarus, come forth." Enter into the expectant pause right before he calls out. Just imagine him gathering energy. He is taking authority over death itself, to call his very dead friend back to life. He is not passive. Though he wept before, his soul carries no grief. Instead he is girded for battle – confident, assured, not even in doubt about laying down the power he has learned so well to take up. For Jesus manifests the same force that created the universe. He flings out the galaxies ever-expanding. Come closer to that energy as the resonance builds in his voice to call out: "Lazarus, come forth!"... Where are you in this moment? What do you experience?

6. [*Pause until 16:00 minutes.*] And now experience one last scene... It is just before daybreak. No one is around. It's after the resurrection. As the sun rises upon the water, Jesus walks along the beach. His disciples are offshore, not too far, in a fishing boat. They've been out all night and have caught nothing. Jesus will talk with them about that, and help them. But in this moment he is completely alone. Can you envision the Christ, who died and rose from death? ... He bends down on one knee, arranging some wood he has been gathering, to build a fire on which he will cook fish for breakfast. He has a familiar recognizable body. Yet nothing like it has ever been. Can you see him? ... His body was born, it has lived. It has been scourged and crucified. It has risen from death. It is human. He moves with a lightness that defies gravity, and yet his feet still feel the crunch of Galilean sand he has known since childhood... He seems calm, like one who has finished almost everything. He looks up into the morning light. He celebrates it...He is complete in every way - full of power and yet not needing to do anything - full of love, and yet not needing to be embraced. He is in time; and he is out of time... He is ever-present. He is now. It is this Jesus who abides with us. He comes to us as we gather together, when

we seek him, and in the Bread and Wine of the Eucharist… He is the source of peace, joy and love. It is this Jesus who has poured out his Spirit upon us, and lives deep within our spirits, when we make a place for him. [*Brief pause*]

Thinking back, which of these six scenes was most interesting, challenging, compelling or comforting? In which one would you like to spend some more time? [*Brief pause*]

Now, as the music continues, take a few moments to capture and expand on paper the scene you have chosen. What significance does it have for your life right now?

[*The recording should have been playing approximately 20 minutes now. "Appalachian Spring" ends quietly as it began at about 25:39 minutes.*]

Now share what you have written around the table. [*Allow about 30 minutes.*]

(Of course, this meditation may also be experienced privately with questions elaborated in the journal.)

+++++++++++

To the Leader: Other music may be used for this long meditation. Something more neutral, not necessarily in the classical style, could provide a less intrusive background, but still give a sense of private space to encourage envisioning. A distinctly Christian piece would be P. Tchaikovsky/ Mozart, "Ave Verum" from "The Mozartiana Suite"… If using other music, one should plan for pauses, especially giving time at the end of each scene.

AFTERWARD: THE RATIONALE

The glory of God is the human person fully alive;
and the life of humanity is the vision of God
~St Irenaeus~

Some of the assumptions in this book about developing a deep and fully human life have a very long history. It was the second generation of Christians who collected the traditions of this new spiritual way in defiance of attitudes and ideas that would cause the Christian movement to veer away from its essence and effectiveness. Evidence of these leaders and their concern for truly representing the spirituality of Jesus is easy to find in the New Testament. But there were other "Apostolic Fathers," and slightly later "Apologists" who are not quite so well known as the eyewitnesses. Some of their writings have also come down to us. Of special importance for the work at hand were the ideas of the 2nd Century defender of the faith, Irenaeus of Lyons. He was a cosmopolitan person from the Roman Imperial period, a time of universal culture and language (*koine* Greek). Communication was not instantaneous as it is for us; still, ideas and goods spread as never before around the Mediterranean basin. It was an era in some ways like our own.

Raised in Asia Minor, Irenaeus became shepherd to a missionary flock in Vienne, near Lyons- a large and prosperous city the Romans called Lugdunum, the center of Celtic Gaul at the confluence of the rivers Rhone and Saone. The Christians of this area were mostly Greek speakers, though there were surely some who spoke Latin, the administrative language. There is evidence that Christianity made only slight impact at this time on the native pagan Celts.[19] But Irenaeus' influence was felt in Rome. And his writings against false Christianity were spread everywhere among the churches. Irenaeus intended to describe and transmit what he called a "Rule of Faith," basically a summary of essential Christian teaching- a bridge, on comparison, between the apostolic witness of the New Testament and what later, in the face of different controversies, was to become creedal orthodoxy . Though Irenaeus' writings no longer exist in a Greek original, a

---

[19] Irenaeus refers to the local pagans as barbarians. And the listing of the "Martyrs of Lyons," dating from about 177, includes only Greek and a few Roman names.

scrap of a Greek manuscript was discovered in the Egyptian desert (among the Oxyrrinchus Papyri). This fragment dates from the author's lifetime, and shows the extent and immediacy of his influence.

The Second century world was spiritually diverse and creative. Even among Christians there began to be accommodation and innovation as the new religion spread in the fermenting spiritual climate historians have labeled "Gnosticism." (This ancient, speculative spirituality has re-emerged among the popular spiritual options of our own time.) It became necessary for Christians to reflect on their vibrant spiritual life, and to create doctrinal boundaries for what was seen as a straight and narrow path grounded in the eyewitness accounts of Jesus' original chosen companions. The apostolic Twelve and other disciples who knew Jesus in the flesh were becoming beloved memories. More and more their letters and collected memoirs became authoritative. The canonical scriptures as we know them were sorted out among the organizing churches of the Second century.

Religious communities spread with commerce along the roads and shipping lanes of the Empire. And Christians defined an emerging world religion in the process, usually in the face of opposition, or what turned out to be false teaching. Christianity increased rapidly during this period, though until the mid-Fourth century it was considered illegal and was subject to periodic persecutions that both kept the traditions pure, and created those heroic exemplars of faithfulness at all costs –the "noble army of martyrs." During the age of martyrs it would be difficult to imagine anyone becoming a Christian with less than intense commitment to a clearly defined spiritual path. It could be said, that this era was the high period of powerful Christian spirituality, before the long centuries of political involvement and compromise, and the cycles of corruption and reform that characterize Christian history. The age of Irenaeus was closer to the pure source of the living water Christ promises to all who thirst. To be a Christian could never be a cloak of respectability or a religious veneer placed upon an otherwise ordinary life. And so, early Christianity was always transformative. It was a spirituality which raised adherents into "fullness of life" in anticipation of the completion of God's plan. (They still believed the second coming of Christ was just around the corner.)

It is not that Christian spirituality was different in the face of persecution. It just became more focused and powerfully alert, like a musician at a performance rather than practicing. At different points of Christian history the spirit of martyrdom was cultivated, but in fact martyrdom was not very likely to occur. This had the result of sustaining a church culture that encouraged speedy purification from concerns and distractions that have no ultimate value. Spiritual development moved right along with the elevated sense of its urgency.

Irenaeus is said to have been a martyr, though this may be a legendary attribution of a later generation of Christians in Gaul. That he lived during the persecutions of the year 177 is certain. The Bishop of Lyons, a man in his 90's, was arrested and died in prison. Irenaeus, from a nearby community, seems to have inherited official responsibility and was sent with an account of these stressful events, which he may have written, to the Christians in Rome. The story of the Martyrs of Lyons is recorded in the 4th Century *Church History* of Eusebius. It reveals a new heroic ideal, universal and egalitarian, one that even the threat of death could not defeat. One of the martyrs was an exemplary witness of great power being both a slave and a woman, characterized in Eusebius as "a tiny, weak and easily ignored woman." This Blandina inspired every one near her in death, like ordinary soldiers sometimes have done in combat. The letter Irenaeus carried to Rome naturally displays some of his own spiritual emphasis in this situation. The Holy Martyr's last hours revealed "she had put on Christ, the great unconquerable athlete, and had routed the adversary in many bouts and had on account of her contest been crowned with the crown of incorruptibility."[20] "Incorruptibility" here suggests a substance like gold so highly refined by fire as to be pure, incapable of further change, and not needing it. Thus is revealed a perfected human life that even death cannot destroy.

Such an athletic and indomitable spirituality was at the heart of Irenaeus' thinking. His model from boyhood was Polycarp, a renowned martyr who died as the 85 year old Bishop of Smyrna. (The fascinating account of his trial and death is easily accessible.) This venerable Christian leader had lived in Ephesus and heard the teaching of the Apostle John and other eyewitnesses of Jesus' ministry. It was this community in the Roman province of Asia that preserved the teaching of "the beloved disciple." This John was the one who described with such depth of reflection the splendid

---

[20] Eusebius, *Church History*, V, 1:41-42

life of the Word who was God, who became man to bring life to the world.

Imbibing this tradition so close to its source gave Irenaeus both authority and focus. He was passionate to share and preserve what is essential to the life-enhancing gospel of Jesus. In the midst of the 2nd Century's religious diversity, its exploding creativity and spiritual subjectivism, Irenaeus stood for something he (and most other Christians) considered to be the straightforward essence of the "truth that can set one free." At the same time that he researched the doctrines and developed arguments against those strands of Gnosticism infecting the churches, he also lived the life of a peacemaker, as *irenic* in behavior as his name suggests he might be. Irenaeus was not only effective as a spiritual guide and witness in his own day. He continues to speak to Christians centuries later. Some of his ideas are foundational for assumptions on which the present work is based. His theological understanding of human nature and destiny may be as useful in the 21st Century as they were to the 2nd.

At the climax of an argument about God's self-expression in the Word made a human person, Irenaeus proclaims the Creator's purpose now plainly (and famously) expressed: "The glory of God is the human person fully alive, and the life of humanity is the vision of God."[21] The unfolding of this theme is the intent of the spiritual pursuit outlined in the reflections, meditations and probing questions of this book. Of course, Irenaeus' understanding cannot easily be transferred into modern thinking about the human personality. But there is an evocative resonance with us in his enthusiasm and positive regard for human potential. And his assumption that the depths of human personality in union with God are truly open to us is inspiring for those who would pursue the work at hand. The ancient witness of Irenaeus still encourages young and old of all eras to persevere in response to the plan God has embedded in our very nature. We can be assured that God has truly become one with us through the Word. There is a redemptive principal located within creation and specified in the historic Jesus, who is still "becoming flesh." By this means, the purpose of our individual being will be brought nearer to completion. Our effort should be to cooperate with the process and not to wander in a spiritual fog, or lose the way by being distracted.

The meaning for Irenaeus of "The glory of God –the human person

[21] *Adversus haereses*, IV, 20:7, translation of Mary Ann Donovan, page 97

fully alive," is best understood from his youthful grounding in the Ephesian church tradition taught by his mentor Polycarp. The Gospel of John portrays the human Jesus both as God's glory made manifest and as life-bringer. He is the Word, God's eternal self-expression. And he is a tangible, en-fleshed human being. In John's gospel, Jesus is both ordinary person and divine being. The same person can be weary and thirsty in the heat of noonday, for example, and still have food to eat which is sustenance quite beyond the disciples' understanding.[22] This Jesus is both a normal man and more than man. He desires to relate in the usual way of human persons, and yet he always manifests the divine among those he encounters. In this tradition to be hospitable to the greater life is always a challenge. He offers not a threat but a promise to **as many as receive him**[23] - both **abundant life**, now[24] and an **eternal life** beyond the tomb.[25]

Irenaeus develops the point about this "life" being from the beginning of creation and traces its development as the agenda revealed throughout the story of salvation (the scriptures), and the story of each person as well. He uses the rhetorical concept of *economy* to point to a thoughtful plan God continually weaves through life, like the recurring themes of a well-designed argument. For history to succeed, no rethinking was needed. Even with the gift (and burden) of spiritual freedom, there is always a reason to be optimistic about human possibilities. Compared to Irenaeus, later theologians were essentially pessimistic: St. Augustine in the West, and St. Athanasius in the East. But in this earlier time, Irenaeus proclaims the essential goodness of the material world and history. And so he emphasizes the positive nature of the complete human being –fleshly body, as well as soul and spirit.

Modern scholars have especially pointed to Irenaeus' refreshing idea of human nature: "Adam was created as a *little one* by a God who always intended that he should grow into the full stature of Christ."[26] Though there was a Fall, and disobedience is still part of being creatures who foolishly have become our own worst enemy, it would be better to consider sin a

---

[22]Both situations are carefully noted in John, Chapter 4 - part of the plot to be explained.

[23]John 1:12

[24]John 10:10

[25]John 12:1-53. Note in verse 40, the connection between receiving this life and "the glory of God."

[26]Denis Minns OP, op.cit., page 136

profound misstep, but not an abysmal fall. "Careful study of Irenaeus has the potential to inject the Christian Church with the fullness of life appropriate to a new millennium."[27]

The 2nd Century Christian way of thinking spiritually is epitomized by Irenaeus; he does not anticipate or require all the turmoil and controversy that will come as history unfolds. He develops concepts used by others of his day to connect ideas in the broad and complex tapestry of the scriptures. In this way he provides a useful, realistic and winsome understanding of the possibility of "the human person fully alive." The concept he uses to organize all this is a common technical term from the teaching of rhetoric at the time: *recapitulation*.[28] This is antiquity's schooled way of pulling together an argument. The word occurs metaphorically in Ephesians (1:10), where it is said Jesus came from the heavens "to recapitulate all things." Irenaeus builds on this symbolic resonance in his own exposition. This rhetorical convention, common in the Imperial Roman thought world, is difficult for translators to put in a few words. But the implication is that history is not moving into what is novel. It is restoring the past. Purpose, as it were, moves both backwards and forwards in time. The Spirit of Truth is literally *educating*, drawing forth what is hidden within. There is in this a wave-like interpenetration of time and eternity. In such a way what is invisible from time to time is made visible, like a dolphin broaching the surface of the sea. God has built into all personal life, a corrective factor, which with awareness can be released, somewhat like a time release medication, as a spiritual balm.[29]

Irenaeus uses *recapitulation* not so much as a technique of writing, in which he seems little interested. It has become, for him, a theological key-word, a metaphor for how God is manifested in creation. Here is a typical passage: "He *recapitulated* humanity in himself, the invisible becoming visible, the incomprehensible being made comprehensible, the impassible becoming capable of suffering, and the Word being made a human being,

---

[27]Mary Ann Donovan, SC, op.cit. Page 174 –This is her conclusion after twenty years of teaching and research in patristics.

[28]In rhetoric, *anakephalaiosis* means a "summing up." For example, in Theophilus, self-consciously: "I will not shrink from summing up for you …the antiquity of our writings." For this and further technical discussion see Grant, *op.cit.,* page50.

[29]"So put away all malice and all guile and insincerity and envy and all slander. Like newborn babes, long for the pure spiritual milk, that by it you may grow up to salvation; for you have tasted the kindness of the Lord." I Peter 2:1-3

summing up all things in himself"[30] Luke, in particular notes, to summarize the birth and infancy stories, that the incarnate Word did not arrive fully mature, like Athena from the head of Zeus. Jesus developed in the normal way of humans –and not just physically. **Jesus *increased* in wisdom and stature (or years), in favor with God and man** (Luke 2:52). This means that like us, Jesus developed fully as a human person, by stages and in relationship with others. Irenaeus interprets, and extends this as a *recapitulation* where Jesus enters redemptively into each phase of human development. He corrects and perfects the whole human life cycle. In order to point out Jesus' involvement, Irenaeus delineates five stages from infant to child, to adolescence to manhood and finally to the elder.[31]

"Jesus sanctifies every age by its resemblance to himself...not rejecting nor surpassing man. For he came to save all through himself –all I say who through him are regenerated into God, infants, children, boys, young men and elders. Therefore he passed through every age, and became an infant for infants, sanctifying the infants; a child among children, sanctifying all of that age, at the same time being made an example for them of piety, righteousness and obedience. Among the young men he was a young man, becoming an example for young men, sanctifying them for the Lord. So also he became an elder among the elders so that he might become a perfect master in every particular, not only in the exposition of the truth, but also in the matter of age, thereby sanctifying the elders and becoming an example to them. Then he passed to his death, so that he might be 'the first begotten from the dead.'"[32]

This passage gives a good example both of Irenaeus' style and thinking. But it seems bizarre to us when later on, he seeks to establish that Jesus must have died at age 49; since this was the age he would need to have reached in order to be considered a wise elder –that is, a fully mature person. Modern historians who place Jesus' ministry at about three years in length and his age 33 at death would judge this to be not a theological but

---

[30] *Adversus haereses*, III, 16:6. Italics added to accent the point being made.

[31] His understanding of the "ages of man" is of course that of his age. Hippocrates mentions these five stages defined by multiples of the number 7. One is a child from one to seven, when the teeth are lost. An adolescent has a trace of beard at 21, and becomes a young man whose body matures at 28. The elder becomes an old man from age 56 (*De septenario, 5)* It is not surprising that human development be described in cultural terms that are obsolete. Perhaps this frees us to consider seriously our own popular culture that creates such distinctions as Generation X, Gen Y and the Millennials, and recently describes 65-75 as the young -old, 75-85 as the old and 85 up as the old-old.

[32] *Adversus haereses,* II,22:4

psychological issue. Jesus certainly died as a young and vigorous man after a short, intense ministry. The ancient cultural view of the stages of life is not something we should be much concerned about.

We are compelled however, to take seriously the cultural changes we are still experiencing, as fresh moments of grace. Adolescence, for example, has different meanings and duration in different parts of the modern world, and is clearly different from ancient views. Most people live longer life spans. The eternal Word still enters to redeem and transform each of these culturally unique scenarios, and no doubt other human possibilities beyond those so far known. The current scientific views about human development and psychological transitions and phases are the basis for understanding spiritual development in this book. That Jesus died as a young man causes us to look farther a-field for images of the Incarnation of the Word recapitulating the divine plan in the whole range of human experience. In the New Testament, Simeon and the octogenarian Anna, and just beyond it, the aged martyr Polycarp, are images of maturity in the spiritual life cycle. These figures too represent the archetype of Christ.

Also, beyond the conceptual purview of Irenaeus, it is important to know how the image of God continues to be manifest redemptively within the couple relationship in the sacrament of Holy Matrimony.[33] Though Jesus was a single man, and the monastic ideal has its place reflecting the inherently solitary condition of humanity, there is for most people a continuing incarnation in the faithful living out of the vows capable of redeeming the "image of God" conceived as a holy couple. Nothing could be more helpful just now than to affirm once again the inherent holiness of the marital union. Mary and Joseph represent this image in the New Testament, and from documents slightly beyond this period, traditional representatives are the parents of Mary, Anne and Joachim whose example of sanctity we consider in the chapter about couples.

The living Word of God, still following Irenaeus' line of thinking, has entered fully into the human condition. He continues to bring fullness of life to all who will receive him throughout the range of human development and in diverse cultures. This is an extension of the rich concept of *recapitulation* which Irenaeus of Lyons began to explore. God has woven the essential

---

[33] So God created man in his own image, in the image of God he created him; male and female he created them (Genesis 1:27).

corrective factor into the human story from the beginning in such a way that freedom of choice and genuine creativity are always part of the picture. Without Irenaeus, we would search far for such a broad concept of spiritually grounded personality, one that permits the corrective and enhancing factor, the Holy Spirit, to enter the human story in each developmental phase.

Rhetorical thinking is a good clue. Take for example, a tragic plot. We can make an overview of the writer's script and find a clear answer every time to the question, "Where did things begin to go wrong?" The writer always conceives a tragedy from a point before the plot manifests the doomed outcome. And so the broad sweep of scripture reveals many "tragic" subplots. But still, the focus of our attention should be on the corrective factor or intervention of grace. The ultimate unfolding will be glorious redemption. Following the 2nd Century mindset, Irenaeus thinks this way, always pointing out in the sweeping course of the Biblical story, how the Word incarnate corrects initial errors in order to avert subsequent disaster. For example, in his interpretation, Christ and Mary (as new Adam and Eve) return to the paradisal garden to correct disobedience by obedience, slavery by liberation, alienation by reconciliation, corruption by incorruption.

It is a basic assumption for these chapters in spiritual development, for which we gratefully acknowledge Irenaeus, that there is great hope for being "fully alive" now. In whatever phase of our experience, we should be able to discover this redemptive and uplifting factor. It is hidden in the depths of our very being awaiting our return. By exercising whatever freedom we have, we may cooperate with God's purpose to make us vibrant and whole. And so our encounter with the deep places of the spirit will require a realistic, yet positive view of human nature. Not everything within is pretty. Courage and perseverance will be called for. Still at bottom, the depth of our personhood is "the image of God," created to be good and capable of restoration at every broken point, more and more to manifest the changeless vitality of the Christ within each person.

Let us now consider the second portion of the maxim from Irenaeus. If, *"the life of humanity is the vision of God,"* the way to fullness is to focus on God. This means we must look in faith (**darkly**, I Corinthians 13), because by definition God is not visible. Yet there is something substantial about small but frequent acts of faith that strengthen the inner person, like muscles responding to resistance exercise. Faith developed is a way of knowing what is otherwise unknowable. It is **the assurance of things hoped for, the conviction of things not seen.**[34] We must stay on the road which is a faith journey; on it, the vision of God is always the destination. Faith, therefore, is to seek the vision and trust what God provides to sustain the journey.

The "vision of God" in Irenaeus' lexicon has two sources, primarily the teaching of Jesus: **Blessed are the pure in heart, for they shall *see* God** (Matthew 5:8); but also, **No one has ever *seen* God; the only Son, who is in the bosom of the Father, he has made him known** (John 1:18).[35] The second source is the cultural view of the Greek world, infused for centuries with Platonic thinking, in which by definition God is invisible. Irenaeus speaks clearly then within his own period. Within a modern cultural understanding, one can say this early Christian points us to three complementary meanings. That is, **"The life of humanity is the vision of God"** means:

1. To be more vital is to stretch out toward what is not visible. God will always be beyond us, the Truth that liberates us to perceive what is beyond self and culture.

2. Therefore, to be more vital is gradually to see all things from God's point of view, in dialogue with revelation from beyond, made concrete by acts of faith.

3. And ultimately, to be more vital is to move toward what is now impossible, to behold God as Jesus does; for, he is the way to the Father.

In order to bridge the gap between the *vision* and experienced *life*, God has placed within us his own Spirit.[36] Something of God is in the depths of every human being. This is why experiences of the divine so often seem familiar, like a "homecoming." Let us call this capacity the *archetype of the*

[34]Hebrews 11:1

[35]Note also the conversation with Philip, John14:8-11.

[36]There is no distinction in Irenaeus between the Holy Spirit and the human spirit, which should perhaps be thought of as "the capacity for God," like a balloon, capable of inflation.

human person. This is the experience the Apostle Paul may have been pointing to when he affirmed: "Christ in me is the hope of Glory." When we enter prayerfully the depths of our being, the *Christ Archetype* emerges with divine power to create, restore and fulfill. And this numinous inner image will correspond with whatever phase of development is in process. Further, this correspondence relates not only to chronological development, the human life cycle. The archetype is non-temporal and so impinges on our experience from outside time to touch current issues. Like Nicodemus in the New Testament (John 3), older people also have times for rebirth, returning to the mother's womb is not the point at all. At many moments pregnant with possibility, we can return to the infant archetype of the divine child for insights and the grace of renewal. Jesus not only participates in each phase of human development, he calls us to participate in his transcendent reality.

In using the language of archetypes we have departed from our first spiritual mentor St. Irenaeus, and moved on to the thought realm of the mid-twentieth century. The pioneering work of the Swiss psychiatrist Carl Jung is the other great mentor whose thinking informs this book. In his work spirituality and psychology fit like hand and glove. Jung's explorations of the unconscious depths through analytical psychology expand on the motivational theories of his teacher, Sigmund Freud, who was convinced the human personality was driven by largely unconscious inner energies – sexuality (or *libido*), aggression and ultimately a will to self-destruct (or *thanatos*). He thought these deep motivators had been largely redirected by the centuries old process of civilization, and with this emerges the conscious self that individuals bring to the table of adult life. But these ambitious ventures in edification have been risky, like building on a swamp which could never sustain a lasting habitation. His classic essay <u>Civilization and Its Discontents</u>, as well as the familiar theory of neurosis, shows Freud's basic pessimism. Religion for him was ultimately an illusion, and so "spirituality" can have no real depth.

His younger disciple Carl Jung, however, thought Freud's theory was too limited to account for the wide range of experience that he studied dispassionately with a phenomenological approach. Over a life time of studies, collected in the multi-volume Bollingen Series, Jung influenced every discipline from psychotherapy to folklore, cinema and religion with his ideas about the deep workings of the personal unconscious - and especially about the collective unconscious, the specifically spiritual dimension with its symbolic manifestations.[37] Freud's understanding of the human depths was pessimistic. The journey of life (and civilized history itself) would have to be like Joseph Conrad's hero moving out into the "pre-civilized" dimension of human experience, only to discover within himself, as the title has it, "The Heart of Darkness." Jung's broader view of the inner world from which conscious life emerges is far more positive because he explored additional spiritual motivators deep in the personality. He studied phenomena as far-ranging as <u>The Tibetan Book of the Dead</u> and the meaning of Medieval theories of alchemy to pursue twin goals of wholeness for the fragmented *self* (inner integration), and the development of the unique character of each life (Jung's term was *individuation*).

This second task especially, engages more than the concerns of a healthy emotional life; there is a spiritual path to be pursued for the development of authentic human personality. A way to move along with this task would be to reflect analytically with a therapist on the inner experience. This process obviously overlaps with spiritual direction of a sort, and may be part of the journey for those who use the chapters of this book. It was Jung's view that spiritual development could not really begin to move forward in our culture until mid-life when there would be more time to devote to the inner journey, and when the approach of physical aging called attention to ultimate concerns. (It should be noted that since Jung himself grew into a pantheistic world-view; his spirituality was not orthodox Christianity. Though many, including this author, have incorporated some of his intellectual framework, not all "Jungians" would call themselves followers of Christ.)

One of the most influential and useful of Jung's ideas is the concept of the *archetype*. The term is rich in meanings; but to put it simply, the archetypes represent basic, instinctive structures of the human being. We are, according to Jung, hardwired with archetypal energy. This energy is manifest in symbolic forms. The mother archetype, for example, is a

---

[37] For depth psychologists, the mind has a fourfold hierarchy of meaning: The **conscious mind** –self aware, rational, can will and act. It is characterized by the *ego*. The **preconscious** is just "out of mind" – memories, motives, accessible material. The **personal** unconscious stores repressed contents, like traumas, forbidden feelings, primitive or instinctive emotion. The **collective** unconscious is a mental reservoir of themes, symbols, archetypes genetically transmitted, what Jung called "the vast historical storehouse of the human race."

numinous quality that resonates within the being of every particular mother. Our mothers are uniquely themselves; but they are also bearers of *the* mother. One of the archetypes is that of the Self, sometimes known as the Hero, which consists of several phases corresponding to the several periods of human development: the infant, child, youth, adult and elder. We meet these characters in different guises in myths, legends, stories, dramas –and not least, in our personal experiences of dreaming, and through meditative reflection on inner imagery, our own and that of others.

In the chapters of this book, we use a Jungian approach to work with our archetypal experience, becoming aware of what is, for many persons, largely unconscious deeper levels of the personality. At the spiritual level we hope to encounter the energy that shapes and reshapes us. This level is also the point of communion between the self and our creator. The point of contact with God is also the place of redemption. It is where the spiritual life originates, bubbles up into consciousness, and flows out into the fuller life Jesus came to bring. It is, as Irenaeus might put it, where Christ the New Adam recapitulates the plan of salvation in each Christian person.

In this book the sections of reflection and journaling are meant to aid our free assent and cooperation with the ongoing, life-giving work of God in the human personality. St. Paul exhorts the faithful to: **Work out your own salvation with fear and trembling, for God is at work in you, both to will and to work for his good pleasure** (Philippians 2:12-13). Cooperative effort is required; passivity is to be avoided. The expositions of the heroic Christ archetype, and the exercises from the traditional repertoire of Christian practice, present a way to do that work.

Each of these chapters is grounded in some aspect of Carl Jung's analytical psychology, resonant with the hopeful and positive theological convictions of Irenaeus of Lyons. Each section explores New Testament situations that evoke or express what seems to be an archetypal moment of personal development, in a meditative way that assumes the scriptures are *sacramental*. This means the surface of the traditional text is capable of leading the prayerful reader into a genuine and powerful encounter with God. This is the presupposition of the ancient and currently popular practice of prayerful, personal Bible study, *lectio divina*. Though no particular theory of scriptural inspiration is espoused in this book, it is assumed that the words of the Holy Bible may be experienced through the Spirit as a message from God, speaking not just to the thinking mind, but addressing the depths of our personal being. Beginning with the surface details of the passage in its context, we look for ways to enter deeply into the text, and to discover the emotional reactions and spiritual intuitions evoked within us. In short, we are using the scripture as a place of encounter with the living Word of God. In the archetypal moment we will always seek the Spirit of Truth, of which Jesus said: **You will know the truth, and the truth will make you free** (John 8:32).

SELECT BIBLIOGRAPHY

+++++++++

PRAYER, MEDITATION AND JOURNALING

Bunge, OSB, Gabriel: *Earthen Vessels: The Practice of Personal Prayer According to the Patristic Tradition*, transl. Michael Miller (Ignatius Press, San Francisco, 2002).

Hallesby, Ole: *Temperament and the Christian Faith*, (Augsburg, Minneapolis, MN, 1962).

Johnston, William: *The Cloud of Unknowing & the Book of Privy Counselling* (Doubleday, New York, 1973).

Kaisch, Ken: *Finding God: A Handbook of Christian Meditation* (Paulist Press, NY, 1994).

Keating, Charles: *Who We Are Is How We Pray* (Twenty-Third Publications, Mystic, CN, 1989).

Mains, John (1): *Words Into Silence* (Paulist Press, NY, 1981).

Mains, John (2): *Letters From The Heart* (Crossroads, NY, 1982).

Mains, John (3): *Moment of Christ* (Crossroads, NY, 1984).

Mains, John (4): *The Present Christ* (Crossroads, NY, 1985).

McKenty, Neil: *In The Stillness Dancing* (Dorton, Lingman & Todd, London, 1988).

Michael, Chester R./ Norrisey, Marie C.: *Prayer and Temperament: Different Prayer Forms for Different Personality Types* (Open Door Inc., Charlottesville, VA, 1984).

Pennington, M. Basil: *Centering Prayer: Renewing an Ancient Christian Prayer Form* (Doubleday & Company, Garden City, NY, 1966).

Progroff, Ira: *At A Journal Workshop: The Basic Text and Guide for Using the Intensive Journal* (Dialogue House Library, NY, 1975).

Simons, George F.: *Keeping Your Personal Journal* (Paulist Press, NY, 1978).

DREAMWORK

Berne, Patricia H./Savary, Louis M.: *Dream Symbol Work: Unlocking the Energy from Dreams and Spiritual Experience* (Paulist Press, NY, 1991).

Bulkelley, Kelly: *Spiritual Dreaming: A Cross Cultural Historical Journey* (Paulist Press, NY, 1962).

Bosnak, Robert: *A Little Course in Dreams* (Shambala, Boston, 1988).

Haden, Robert L. *Unopened Letters from God: Using Biblical Dreams to Unlock Your Nightly Dreams* (HadenInstitute.com, 2011).

Hillman, James: *The Dream and the Underworld* (Harper & Row, NY, 1979).

Jung, Carl Gustav: *Dreams* (Bollingen Series, Princeton, NJ, 1974.)

Kelsey, Morton: *God, Dreams, and Revelation: A Christian Interpretation of Dreams* (Augsburg Press, Minneapolis, MN, 1991).

Savary, Berne & Williams: *Dreams and Spiritual Growth: A Christian Approach to Dreamwork* (Paulist Press, NY, 1984).

Taylor, Jeremy: *Dreamwork: Techniques for Discovering the Creative Power of Dreams* (Paulist Press, NY, 1983).

ICONOGRAPHY

Baggley, John: *Doors of Perception: Icons and their Spiritual Significance* (SVS Press, Crestwood, NY, 1988).

Coomler, David: *The Icon Handbook: A Guide to Understanding Icons and the Liturgy, Symbols & Practices of the Russian Orthodox Church* (Templegate Publishers, Springfield, IL, 1995).

Forest, Jim: *Praying With Icons* (Orbis Books, Maryknoll, NY, 1997).

John of Damascus, Saint: *On The Divine Images* (SVS Press, Crestwood, NY, 2002).

Nouwen, Henri J.M.: *Behold the Beauty of the Lord: Praying With Icons* (Ave Maria Press, Notre Dame, IN, 1987).

Ouspensky, Leonid/Lossky, Vladimir: *The Meaning of Icons* (Saint

Vladimir's Seminary Press, Crestwood, NY, 1983).

Ramos-Poqui, Guillen: *The Technique of Icon Painting* (Burns & Oates/ Search Press, Turnbridge Wells, UK, 1991).

Sendler, Egon, trans. Steven Bigham: *The Icon: Image of the Invisible* (Oakwood Pulications, Torrence, CA, 1993).

Temple, Richard: *Icons & the Mystical Origins of Christianity* (Luzac Oriental Limited, Oxford, UK, 2001).

Tragido, Alfredo, trans. S. Sartarelli : *Icons and Saints of the Eastern Orthodox Church* The JP Getty Museum, Los Angeles, CA, 2004).

Williams, Rowan: *Ponder These Things: Praying with Icons of the Virgin* (Sheed and Ward, Franklin, WI, 2002).

Zibawi, Mahmoud: *The Icon, Its Meaning and History* (The Liturgical Press, Collegeville MN, 1993).

Made in the USA
Charleston, SC
01 December 2011